IF THEY HAD KNOWN

STUDIES OF
EVERYMAN AT THE CROSS

IF THEY HAD KNOWN

STUDIES OF
EVERYMAN AT THE CROSS

BY

LESLIE F. CHURCH, B.A., Ph.D.

Author of
Oglethorpe: A Study of Philanthropy in England and America
&c.

LONDON
THE EPWORTH PRESS
(EDGAR C. BARTON)
25-35 CITY ROAD, E.C.1

TO

EVERYMAN ON HIS WAY TO THE CROSS

First Edition . . . 1936

Made *and* printed *in* Great Britain
By The Camelot Press Ltd
London *and* Southampton

CONTENTS

E. Keightley.

A present from the Author.

TO THE READER

THE EARLY CHAPTERS of this little book might be called studies in imaginary conversions. They were offered originally to the people of a city Church, and in such a congregation all the characters described were present.

Experience led one to believe that if the 'Hamlets' and the 'Lancelots' could see Jesus they would be transformed, and perhaps transfigured. Such, indeed, proved to be the case.

Whatever may be our theory of the working of salvation, it remains true that no man is saved until he brings his whole life to that love whose 'supreme measurement' is the Cross.

This book makes no pretence at literary criticism or theological analysis. That is not its purpose. It is an attempt to bring the man in the street, with all his imperfection and sin, face to face with Jesus. If such men had known Him!

The contents are arranged so that they may be read, conveniently, in Holy Week.

Needless to say the author is indebted to many writers of great and beautiful books. They will accept his acknowledgement of their gifts, since in this service there must ever be a common treasury.

FOREWORD

EVERYMAN AT THE CROSS

THE FIRST LITERATURE on the Cross of Jesus was nailed to its wood. The author, Pontius Pilate, was not aware of the theological or historical implications of his writing. If he had known the full significance of his statement ' Jesus of Nazareth, King of the Jews,' the subsequent story of mankind might have been written differently.

Long before that day, prophets had foretold the suffering of God. Theologians, long after, have tried to discover and interpret the secret of the Cross. Poets, blessed with insight rather than foresight, have revealed something of its eternal Truth to those who were willing to see.

Meanwhile the vast majority of men pass by in wilful or accidental ignorance.

There is an old stone cross in a Devon market-place where men and women have gathered for centuries. Some have discussed the prices of their wares. Others have come to air their grievances or plight their troth. Not many have even considered the symbolism of the trysting-place at which they met. If they had known—they would not have crucified Him. If they had known—He might have transfigured them.

In a dark hour of the Great War I remember seeing a weary battalion halt by an old, battered wayside Calvary. They flung down their packs and stretched themselves at its base to rest a few moments before they trudged across the mud to the trenches. I can see their tired faces now. Underneath a mask of proud indifference was the strained agony of desperation. The battered cross, I believe, stood for something we all needed that day. If we had known—but we went on twisting our cracked lips into a wry smile and a defiant blasphemy.

This little book is an attempt to stand with Everyman at the Cross and learn its secret. We differ in temperament and opportunity. We are the slaves of many circumstances, but we have thrown down our packs, and we are sick of wearing masks.

Whilst we shall not talk in theological language, we are so desperate that we shall try to find out what we might have known long ago— the difference that Love would make to each of us. There is no unity of time for us. We are just Hamlet or Macbeth, Lancelot or Demas— Everyman at the Cross.

AN ACT OF RECOLLECTION

EVERYMAN'S PILGRIMAGE

As we stand at the Cross, wondering, let us recollect each man his own pilgrimage.

And it came to pass that as I trod that long, uncertain way—feet bleeding, heart breaking—I reached a turn in the road. Beside me loomed a gateway, through which I passed, making bare my very soul to Him who opened the gate to me. His face was marred, whereat I wept, knowing whose blows had wounded Him.

Beyond the gate lay a garden, and presently I rested there, so that my weariness passed away.

So quiet was it in that place that there came a sound of gentle stillness, and, lo, within my hushed spirit, a Voice that called me by my name.

'Behold Me and see—pierced through and through with countless sorrows. Is it nothing to you, O Everyman?'

Then did I know He knew. If I had known before, O Everyman, my brother, we two had never missed our way.

O Saviour of the world, who by Thy Cross and precious blood hast redeemed us, save us and help us, we humbly beseech Thee, O Lord.

I

SIMON PETER

Little love, little trust : but great love brings great confidence.

ROBERT LEIGHTON
1611–1684

Love Him and keep Him for thy Friend, who when all go away will not forsake thee, nor suffer thee to perish in the end.

THOMAS À KEMPIS
1380–1471

And I also say unto thee,
thou art Peter (the rock).

St. Matthew xvi. 18

I

SIMON PETER

Medieval artists assembled many centuries in their pictures of Calvary. Foolish critics have grown querulous because Francis of Assisi and Bernard of Clairvaux lived long after the event and should not have been shown standing with Roman soldiers and Jewish pilgrims who followed the procession to the little hill. The artists were right, for the Cross is an eternal symbol, and all mankind is in its neighbourhood.

There is a crowd, of which we are part, that still watches the Crucifixion and wonders what it really means. Amongst them are the ignorant and the learned, the arrogant and the humble. Some of them do not know and do not care. Others do not know but long to understand. Some cry out, ' One thing I know—the rest I go on to know.' We make a motley crowd, with our little labels proclaiming our beliefs, or our cheap finery which says loudly, ' This man believes in nothing at all '—until the wind stirs the rags and whispers, ' Not even in himself.'

15

Some few there are who have entered into the secret. Let us look at one of these first.

If we are asked to name quickly our favourite disciple, we are a little embarrassed. We feel we ought to say, ' John,' but we want to say, ' Peter.' Why? It is because we are dimly conscious that part of his story is like our own. He is so very human, we say. He is near us in the crowd—some distance from the Cross. Does he know what it means? Shall we ever be able to forget that very unsatisfactory word ' impulsive ' when we think of him?

In a story by Henry James two of the characters discuss a string of pearls which had been bequeathed to one of them by a dead woman. The man is sceptical of their value. They are not genuine! One of the women in his party borrows them, and appears presently, wearing the necklace. The pearls seem transformed. A soft beauty glows in them. ' What have you done to them? ' the guests cry. ' Only handled them, understood them, admired them, and put them on,' she answers. ' That's what pearls are for; that's what they want; they want to be worn; it wakes them up. They're alive, don't you see? How have these been treated? They must have been ignored, buried, despised. They were half dead. Don't you know about pearls? '

There was a transformation, as obvious as that, in the life of Simon Peter. No other man amongst the Twelve is discussed so intimately. He seems to us to be our kinsman in spiritual experience. Some of the earlier moments of his life seem to pronounce judgement on him. He is 'paste'—an imitation—till suddenly the lustreless heart of the man is transformed, like pearls that have been worn by a lover and awakened.

Personality of Simon It is foolish to suggest that he was a weak personality, even in the earlier days. Perhaps the secret of his spiritual struggle lay in the strength rather than the weakness of his nature. If he married the daughter of Aristobulus, that fact is early evidence of his remarkable personality. Her father and her Uncle Barnabas had experienced reverses of fortune. Financial difficulties may have caused their removal from their island home, but its traditions would remain an abiding influence. She would be a lady of culture and refinement, educated in Cyprus, a treasure-house of Greek art. If Peter had been a fisherman of Galilee of weak and vacillating disposition, he would not have married a woman of this type. Even the fact that the family was living in reduced circumstances would not have warranted such a match.

However, the proof of his strong personality does not rest on this speculation. There is ample evidence to show that he was a man of tremendous enthusiasms. This is not fairly described by the word impulsive. Chrysostom is nearer the mark when he says he was ' ever ardent, ever leaping before his fellows.'

Such ardour is usually associated with frankness. The reserve which characterized John was in sharp contrast to the easy familiarity of Simon Peter. Outspoken men pay a price for their candour, and the enthusiasm had its inevitable harvest of mistakes. Never secretive, and seldom silent, the man who has been airily termed impulsive always provided his critics with ample evidence.

There is that moment when Andrew and Simon his brother were washing their nets on the beach. It is one thing to clean your tackle when a good haul of fish is on its way to the market, but it is a very different thing to wash out the weed and the pebbles from nets that have caught nothing else. If you are a good fisherman you will do it and then go, despondently maybe, to bed. That day the crowd pressed Jesus hard. He needed a boat as a vantage-point from which to teach them. There were several there, but He chose Simon's, and there was no argument ! A weak man might have complained.

SIMON PETER

When Jesus had finished speaking to the crowd at the edge of the beach, He turned to this impulsive (!) man who had been so patient, and said, ' Push out into the deep water, and let go your nets for a catch.' Simon looked up astonished, perhaps even exasperated, for his friend was a landsman and he was a fisherman who knew the weather and the prospects only too well. ' Cap'n,' he says, with fisherman's familiarity, ' we've fished all night and got nothing.' It is a natural reproof. Darkness was a good time for the fishing, and he and Andrew had used all the cunning of their experience to no effect. What could this man from Nazareth know ? If they had known the answer to that question—but somehow just then Simon Peter caught a glimpse of it. Maybe Jesus looked at him, for he was ever susceptible to the expression in the face of his Friend. In the middle of his sentence he changes his mind. ' Cap'n, we've fished all night and got nothing, but— a'right, cap'n.' The sequel brings the same full response to a chastened man. There is no apology for his mistake. There is much more. ' Lord,' he cries, and the changed word suggests the sudden fear of undeserved intimacy, ' leave me, for I am a sinful man.' These are not the words of a weak man, nor of a creature of mere impulse.

The same enthusiastic frankness leads to what is often called ' the great confession ' at Cæsarea Philippi. When Jesus wanted to hear the mind of the twelve disciples, He asked them just to tell Him what the people thought of the Son of Man. Then, turning, He said, ' But you, who do you say I am ? ' It is Simon's chance to unburden himself of the great conviction that has been growing stronger every day. ' Thou art the Messiah,' he says, and his eyes flash defiance at the whole world. There is a response, immediate and enthusiastic, from Jesus Himself. ' And I say unto thee, Thou art the Rock.' It is scarcely the designation of a wavering, excitable creature, is it ? Rocks are not impulsive, you say, but neither are they enthusiastic. When enthusiasm is deep-rooted and reliable, when affection is unshakable in spite of all its mistakes, it may be considered rock-like. In that hour the love of Peter made straight the way of Christ to the Cross, but it has been rightly said that the mistakes of that same love sometimes blocked the road.

Scarcely had the enthusiasm of Peter earned him his new name, when he almost belied it. The confession had made it easier for Jesus to tell His friends that He must soon tread the last stretch of His journey which was to end at the Cross. When Peter heard it he was horrified.

' Mercy on Thee, Lord,' he cried, using the vernacular, ' this must not be.' Jesus looked through him to the devil who used his love as a mouthpiece. ' Get behind Me, Satan,' He said. 'You are a hindrance . . .' The loving enthusiasm that had made the road now blocked it. If Peter had known what the Cross meant—but to him it was a hideous threat to the life that began to mean so much.

So Peter appears to me, as I read of his earlier contacts with his Master. I do not think he blew hot and cold by turns. He was consistent from the beginning, but he lacked the quality of reflection. He could not meditate quietly until he was able to take the long view of a situation that had brought him out, with flags flying and drums beating to the attack, with every man in the garrison at one place for one immediate purpose. There is a sentence, written by Augustine of Hippo, which sums up our conclusion at this point. ' If John was the disciple whom Jesus loved, then Peter was the disciple who loved Jesus.' There can be no doubt of that, and he was tempted and tried because he loved.

Tremendous Enthusiasms Amongst a number of incidents which illustrate the first factor in the character of Peter, one must suffice. It occurred when the shadow of the Cross had fallen heavily over the lives of the disciples. Gathered in the Upper Room at that last meal, which was the first of an endless sequence, the friends were perplexed by the action of Jesus.

As they reclined round that table shaped like a horse-shoe, John was at the end of the other arm. When Jesus, girded with a towel, began that ceremonial washing of His friends' feet, He went first to John. The next few minutes were an agony to Peter. The rest apparently submitted without protest, but he watched with growing horror. It was an outrage—at least it would be if he allowed the Master to wash *his* feet.

The ceremony was almost over. Jesus stood before Peter with hands outstretched. The flood of protest bursts into vehement words. 'Lord— Thou—of me washest the feet!' If only he had known what it really meant! 'You will never wash my feet, never!' 'Unless I wash you,' Jesus says, 'you will not share My lot.' Instantly Peter answers, not because he has changed but because he accepts every correction as soon as he understands it, 'Lord, then wash not only my feet but my hands and head.'

There was not much occasion for smiling in those last dread hours, but I feel sure that Jesus smiled then. The complete whole-heartedness of this simple lover was irresistible. There were no subtleties in Simon Peter, and when he was near Jesus no fear of appearing ridiculous restrained his full expression.

With all its risks, it is a quality which might be cultivated in the age in which we live. There is nothing blasé or bored about this man. He tumbles from one mistake to another, but he never ceases to express his love. One remembers the charming passage in Kenneth Grahame's *Dream Days*. Two children are discussing the date. It is October the twenty-first, Trafalgar Day, and the girl, to whom Nelson is a peerless hero, is exasperated that everybody seems to have forgotten. The old gardener is about his ordinary tasks. ' Why can't we *do* something ? ' she cries indignantly, and forthwith gathers a great bundle of pea-sticks and makes a bonfire. What she suffered by way of punishment was nobody's business but her own. Somebody had done something, even if it was the wrong thing ! Inertia is one of the deadliest sins, and veils the Cross more darkly than enthusiasm with all its mistakes.

Perhaps if mankind was as ardent in its desire for peace as was Simon Peter to serve his Lord, ' something would be done by somebody,' even though it meant staking national sovereignty or big business to obtain the result.

Tragic Blunders   This brings us to the tragic focus of the problems of Simon Peter. The shadow from the Cross was more than a shadow now. The dreadful night came in which soldiers and a mob set out to take their prisoner. Peter sees the rabble approaching. Others were petrified with astonishment, or logically convinced that no good could come of resistance. Not so with Simon Peter ! He snatches a sword to die in one last effort to save his Friend. All the rage of the old berserker is in his heart—yet, strangely enough, it is the child of his love. Savagely he slashes out, and the sword takes toll. ' Whereupon Jesus said to Peter, " Sheathe your sword. Am I not to drink the cup which the Father has handed Me ? " ' Commentators have said that Jesus saved Peter's life that night. He had made one more mistake, and I can see him cowering like a great dog which has sprung to defend its master only to be rebuked and brought to heel. It was past his understanding. He did not know. He just loved blindly.

There came at last the hour of his own tragedy. Why did he deny Jesus ? *Because he was there, close by.* That seems a stupid answer, but it happens to be true. Where were the other ten disciples ? Were they hiding from the storm which had broken ? Were they huddled in some room discussing the situation ? Perhaps John was struggling to exert his influence in the household of the High Priest. No man knows these things, but one fact emerges quite clearly. Peter could not keep away. They were trying his Friend, in the dark hours of the night. He was worn and lonely, somewhere in the room above the courtyard. They all said there was nothing to be done. Well, one never knew. He would be as close to Him as he could get, in case of some mad opportunity. He had to be near because he loved Him, so there he stood, forlorn, in the cold darkness of the courtyard.

Mischief lurks in the eyes of a serving-maid. She sees her chance to score a point before the soldiers. Twice she pesters him, and the third time he forgets himself. He is a fisherman again. An oath escapes from his lips. He has denied his Lord.

Some one is looking down on him from that upper room. It is the troubled face of his Friend. At that very moment of all moments He looks at him and breaks his heart. The contact has ended. Peter is out alone in the dark. If he had hidden himself in safety this would never have happened. That is not why he is sobbing out there in the shadows. ' To think that *I* of all men did this ! '

His love and enthusiasm have led him to a

tragic blunder a real coward could not have made. The cowards were not there !

Absolute Tenacity Let us follow him back through the dark streets to his lonely room. I have often wondered what he did during the long hours that lay between his denial and Easter Day. There, in the corners of the room with its haunting mysteries, he would see Jesus, just looking at him. The splendid fact remains—he did not give up.

There is a technical phrase used of the resistance offered to tearing—absolute tenacity. This was the saving grace in Peter. Nothing could tear him away from his beloved Master.

There was no hope that he could undo his terrible mistake. Restitution was an impossibility. Some men would have swung over to the other side. They might have brazened it out with swaggering bravado. They might have hidden the whole circumstance. No one need ever have known !

But Peter is like the boy who gets all his sums wrong, yet turns up in class next day. That had often happened to him. It could not happen any more. The Teacher was on His way to death. The class had broken up !

Still he could not give up. ' I have failed Him just when He needed me most; He knows that I

denied Him. His eyes told me so—but I *do* love
Him. Nothing can alter that. It is too late to
make amends, yet I shall love Him to the end.'

André Maurois said recently, ' In youth every
defeat seems final.' Peter would not admit that
any defeat was final. At any rate no defeat could
force him to surrender his love, which held on
grimly when a thousand voices questioned his
loyalty.

It would be difficult to say when he began to
know the meaning of that Cross. One can share
with him his misery as he realized his own failure
in the crisis. One can enter into his dumb
struggle to believe, in the empty hours between
the Crucifixion and Easter morning. Yet it was
Peter who seemed to grasp as thoroughly as
anyone the reality of the Resurrection. It was
Peter who after the wonder of Pentecost began to
preach passionately the invincible power of the
Risen Christ.

Struggling to reach Jesus on the water he
begins to *sink*, but he does not *drown*. Some one
has used a fine phrase about Peter—' Satan often
tripped him up, but he did not possess him.'

The Under-standing Heart So it came to pass that ' Everyman '
went on to know what he had missed
for so long. Legends have clustered
round the name of ' Peter,' and they are not

without interest. Perhaps he went to Rome towards the end of his life. Some still hold that he went for a while to the Jews in Babylon. Certainly he was as ardent a home missionary as Paul was a foreign missionary. Antioch, Lydda, Joppa, were scenes of his labours. How did this man of primitive emotions get beyond his failure to a new beginning?

Was it because the Cross threw not a shadow but a light upon his heart? All that he could remember of Jesus was lit up by that last complete act of love. He could not give up God because, in this tragedy, he realized God would not give him up.

Perhaps no other disciple had followed Jesus with more dogged devotion through the years. He had an intimate knowledge of His words and works, but now the knowledge became understanding. There was a new synthesis of mind and heart, and it was this last supreme gesture on Calvary which accomplished it.

'Ask what I shall give thee,' said the voice of God to young Solomon as he dreamed of his kingdom. 'Give Thy servant an understanding heart,' was the answer, for which word alone he deserved his reputation for wisdom.

It was just that quality which seems to have come to Peter in his later years. The Hebrew phrase may be translated 'a heart that hearkens.'

The Vulgate suggests 'teachable,' and Luther renders it 'obedient.' These qualities were all part of Simon Peter's personality, but they were not blended until the event on Calvary had transfigured him.

When Peter realized that Jesus loved him far more than he loved Jesus, everything was changed. He saw how blind he had been, and he began to understand his own love in the light of God's love.

The tradition of his passing is too like the truth to be omitted. In that last year he went to Rome, they say. It was a dangerous moment for a Christian leader. The little community begged him to escape. He climbed the wall, but down the road there came a figure whose image was stamped upon his heart. 'Lord, whither art Thou going?' he cried. 'I am come to Rome to be crucified a second time,' the Lord replied. Peter went back. There must be no escaping now. Legend says his wife was martyred first, and he stood, bound, watching one more tragedy. 'Remember the Lord,' he cried out loudly. Then they crucified him, but head downwards as he desired.

We cannot prove this happening. We do not need evidence. Peter had been crucified a thousand times in the years that lay between. However he died, I know he was not afraid deep down in his heart, for perfect love—love upon the Cross for ' Everyman '—had cast out fear.

He looked like a sham jewel, they said, as they looked at him cynically. ' Pearls want to be worn ; it wakes them up. . . . They were half dead. Don't you know about pearls ? '

The heart of Everyman—even when his name is Peter—is a pearl of great price, so great that God gave everything for its redemption.

II

HAMLET

This is the chief significance of the suffering of Christ for us, that we cast all our grief into the ocean of His suffering. If thou sufferest only regarding thyself, from whatever cause it may be, that suffering causes grief to thee, and is hard to bear. But if thou sufferest regarding God and Him alone, that suffering is not grievous nor hard to bear, because God bears the load. The love of the Cross must swallow up our personal grief. Whoso does not suffer from love, for him sorrow is sorrow and grievous to bear; but whoso suffers from love he sorrows not, and his suffering is fruitful in God.

MEISTER JOHANNES ECKHART
1260–1327

*The pain God is allowed to
guide ends in a saving repentance never to be regretted,
whereas the world's pain
ends in death.*

2 COR. vii. 10 (Moffatt)

II

HAMLET

IN MY PICTURE of Everyman at the Cross there
are strange neighbours. Near Simon Peter, so
essentially a man of action as to be almost
thoughtless, stands Hamlet, who gets so little
done because he thinks so much. Even the purpose he struggles to accomplish is thwarted, and
he is left lying on a stage strewn with the wreck-
age of his own hopes and the bodies of those
with whom he struggled blindly.

Who is Hamlet? No one has answered the
question better than William Hazlitt. ' Whoever
has become thoughtful and melancholy through
his own or others' mishaps, whoever has borne
about the clouded brow of reflection, whoever
has known the pangs of despised love, whoever
has had hopes blighted and youth staggered by
strange visions, whoever has had the powers of
action eaten up by thought, whoever has felt

CK   33

the universe infinite and himself nothing '—
that is he. Hamlet is but a name. It is we who
are Hamlet.

Take such a man in such a mood and face him
with the Cross of Jesus. What happens? What
would have happened to Hamlet if he had
known?

There is so much in our life to-day that is
Hamlet-like, and because of this there is a kind
of sincerity which ends by being strangely ineffective. It wanders vaguely on what should
be a journey towards a goal. Sometimes it
shrinks from sudden issues in a morbidity which
looks remarkably like cowardice. It avoids discipline, because it imagines all disciplinary exer-
cise is performed in grim solitude. In the end
it sinks into mawkish despair, whispering, ' What
is the use of anything? '

When youth feels itself at the mercy of a complex system of contrary forces, it too often
becomes resigned to the functionless existence
of a bubble on a stream that strains to burst the
dam. It surrenders. What steps have led to
this moral disaster? So many of the dramatists
and pseudo-philosophers of our age are prepared
to accept the position as inevitable, or to smother
the answer under the ambiguous phrase ' the
post-war age.'

There is only one place, it seems to us, at

which Hamlet could find purpose amidst such chaotic forces. As he struggles up the little hill, and falls exhausted at the foot of the Cross, he may discover the stupidity of his own mistakes. That of itself would be a desolating experience, but even as he learns the truth about himself he may discover the truth about God. With that revelation would come the end of his aimless wandering and the beginning of his adventurous pilgrimage.

To see this possibility we must know what type of man Hamlet was—what sort of person your Hamlet is !

The Greatest Egotist In some ways he is the greatest egotist in the world. He is convinced that on his spare shoulders rests the destiny of a section of mankind. He must do God's work as well as his own. Above all things he is problem-conscious.

Shakespeare shows us a youth for whom life is stark tragedy. His father, slain by his mother's lover, appears in ghastly form to reveal the truth to the distracted boy. Hamlet swears to avenge him. Speaking to his friend Horatio, he says :

> The time is out of joint : O cursed spite
> That ever I was born to set it right.

But no man is saddled with such tremendous destiny. Here, at the very beginning, we go

35

wrong, like Hamlet. We look, not at a stage, but at a world with greed and lust successfully sustained by the petty intrigues of individuals or the complex subtleties of international jealousies. Almost unconsciously we look at the situation as isolated units and, with unbelievable egotism, assume that we were born to set it right. Of ourselves we can do but little. It is small wonder that, with such a beginning, we conclude at last that we can do nothing.

When Everyman considers the meaning of the Cross, he ceases to be an egotist even in good works !

Some time ago I remember talking with a man who longed for what he called 'inward peace.' He was willing to fulfil most of the conditions which experience proves to be essential. One thing prevented his acceptance. Two years before, his brother had deeply wronged him. By a tissue of lies he had created so strong a case against him that he had been arrested and sentenced to a term of imprisonment. It seemed clear that the crime had been committed by this treacherous brother. The man's home had been broken up, and I found him derelict in a drab street in South London. Over and over again he said to me, 'I can't forgive my brother. I can't forgive him, and so I shall never be at peace again.' You see the heart of his problem ! Of course he couldn't forgive him, for the *sin* was against God, and forgiveness was not an isolated human concern. When he and I knelt together at the foot of the Cross, everything was different. All the egotism of personal revenge passed ; the Crucified and he, in one miracle of co-operative love, came to the forgiving. Therein lay peace.

But Hamlet did not know ! He attempted the impossible, alone. Neither the death of Claudius or Gertrude would have been a complete act of justice. He batters away against circumstance and falls back, baffled and bleeding.

The next stage is inevitable. His latent melancholy becomes morbidity. He is tempted to end everything. Life has become spiritless and futile. The world's pain may well end in death. He has lost his faith in men—even in life itself. Hamlet is ' outside life and cannot get into it . . . the baffling of Fate leads to slack water between tides,' says John Masefield.

Brooding over one's own futility, life becomes almost sterile, and the ultimate and only child of unrelieved melancholy is death. We are such egotists, ourselves, that we sit alone, or in groups and councils, considering how *we* can put things right. Circumstances beat us, and they always will, for God's plan includes God. We leave Him out. We were born to set things right. We fail, and over go our groups, our councils, our leagues—because we have hurled ourselves at circumstance and been toppled over in ignominious defeat.

The The first mood—which is not vulgar
Cipher arrogance but rather an uninformed egotism existing unintentionally in well-meaning hearts—passes. In defeat the egotist becomes a cipher. I, who a moment ago was born to set things right, am nothing.

Hamlet feels himself the sport of circumstance. He is half a fatalist now. He speaks to his friend again.

> There are more things in Heaven and earth, Horatio,
> Than are dreamt of in your philosophy.

If only he had known that one of the things missed out was a Cross ! If he could have seen the heart of Him who hung upon it ! But he does not know. Sometimes we feel he is creeping near the fringe of the mystery.

> There's a divinity that shapes our ends,
> Rough-hew them as we will.

He sees something vaguely moving in the shadows, but it is a monster, not a Christ.

There is an old story, ascribed to many artists, of a master painter who gave his students an idea and left them. Presently he would return and look at their crude efforts to express it. He would take his brush and change a line here and there, until a child's attempt became a masterpiece.

In Hamlet's semi-fatalism there is no glad expectation of such divinity. The hand has a moving finger such as Omar Khayyám saw. It does not transfigure our efforts. It destroys them.

The schoolboy who rewrote the lines and changed their punctuation was a Hamlet in embryo. His version went, ' There's a divinity that shapes our ends rough. Hew them as we will.'

The semi-fatalism which is typical of much in what is called the modern outlook leads to vacillation. Hamlet becomes ineffective. He suffers much because he vacillates much. There is a strange inability to rule Providence out altogether, but he sees it working as an inexorable Fate. He asks, in the mood of to-day, ' What's the good of it all ? ' The tragedy is that many a youth, who is a potential Sir Galahad, allows the acid of his intellect to eat away his faith in God and man. From self-sufficient significance he passes to insufficiency and utter insignificance. He can do nothing. The dice are loaded against him, yet somewhere, deep down, there is a Voice which makes him uncomfortable at the thought of hastened death.

39

IF THEY HAD KNOWN

To be or not to be : that is the question :
              To die : to sleep ;
To sleep : perchance to dream : aye, there's the rub ;
For in that sleep of death what dreams may come,
When we have shuffled off this mortal coil,
Must give us pause. . . .
              Who would fardels bear,
To grunt and sweat under a weary life,
But that the dread of something after death,
              puzzles the will,
And makes us rather bear the ills we have
Than fly to others that we know not of ?
Thus conscience does make cowards of us all ;
And thus the native hue of resolution
Is sicklied o'er with the pale cast of thought.

So, as some one has said, he hesitates between morbid inactivity and feverish energy. Presently his life becomes utterly tragic, unrelieved by any faith or hope at all.

The Wrong Target In all this agony of soul there is one outstanding fact. Hamlet is most sorry for himself. He is the centre of the tragedy. Here is the egotist peeping out again. Even when disaster befalls his mother, or Ophelia, or Laertes, it is he who bemoans his fate. He is an unfortunate son or lover or friend. He has a task of vengeance. His father was a pale phantom, past any human aid, but his mother was a blood-stained harlot. Ophelia was bowed beneath her grief and tottering to the terrible darkness. Laertes was beside himself with sorrow. The kingdom was shaken to its foundations. Poor Hamlet gathers all these things to himself, selfishly, and so misses tremendous opportunities. In this self-centredness he loses the royalty of his soul. He is but ' a king of shreds and patches.'

For one moment he has some faint glimmering of what might be. Turning to his mother, the erring queen, he says,

> Confess yourself to Heaven ;
> Repent what's past ; avoid what is to come.

She quivers on the edge of deliverance, as she answers him,

> O Hamlet, speak no more,
> Thou turn'st mine eyes into my very soul.

At that crisis he failed her, and failing her, failed the father he sought to avenge, failed himself and failed the God who made them living souls. Life seemed tragic futility once more.

So youth cries out through the years, ' What's the use of it all ? ' If he had known the love that hung upon the Cross, he would have seen his way out of all his maze of futile effort.

The real tragedy of Hamlet is that he aimed at the wrong target. Nothing mattered if only he could exact vengeance. All round him were people worse than dead ! It never occurred to him that there was any possibility of changing the soul of that poor thing with bloody hands that sat upon the throne. Claudius must be killed—that is the purpose of his life.

There is much talk of friendship in these days. With modern lack of reserve we rush into intimacies that would have seemed impossible fifty years ago. We analyse our loves and hates in the limelight of publicity, instead of the secrecy of our personal laboratories. This in many ways is an advantage, but when friendship counts for much, the friend must be prepared to face the crisis.

There come circumstances which baffle human love. What then? No man is justifying his affection unless he has explored every possibility of befriending his friends. He cannot be content to say, ' So far will I go with you, but there will come occasions when I can do no more. You will slip away in the darkness, and I shall have to let you go into the jaws of death. My friendship stops there, at the edge of the mystery. I do not believe in prayer or God or immortality.'

It may be that, in the language of to-day, the friend will ' let you down.' What then? You will seek to be revenged? Or, with a mawkish complacency, you will do nothing.

When such a Hamlet seeks the Crucified, he learns that love never gives up, even on the

42

Cross. He says, ' This Being who made me capable of love has not built a wall of darkness that is impenetrable. There is no death.' To the treacherous heart of his friend, he does not say, ' I will break you,' nor can he say, ' I will leave you alone.' In the shadow of the Cross he says, ' I have learned that love has no boundaries. God who teaches me forgiveness, will show me His salvation for my friend.'

Philosophers and politicians look at war and wonder how it can be avoided. Some rake up an ancient piece of machinery which is suspiciously like the ' balance of power ' and urge humanity to a peace established on a see-saw whose occupants are for ever shuffling out of position. Some shriek for bigger armies and navies, with more aeroplanes, so that other people may be frightened off. They may quarrel and destroy outside our garden, but we shall live in splendid isolation. Others talk hopefully about collective security, which has much to recommend it, but which can never stand as a permanent method, still less as an ultimate goal.

There is no permanence in peace till men's hearts are changed. Men's minds may be convinced that peace is better than war. What does ' better ' mean ? More profitable, more comfortable, even more sane ? It is a moral issue. When men have learnt that the question is not one of ' better or worse ' but of ' right or wrong,' then peace may reign on earth amongst men of good will.

Machinery may be necessary for immediate results, but it is a soulless thing. Hamlet may imprison the king and queen, or kill them, but the tragedy remains. There is only one solution that is worthy of him at his best. The king and queen must be converted ! One can almost hear the shriek of disapproval at such a suggestion. Is crime to go unpunished ? Is the sentimentalist to overrule the common decencies of justice ?

Justice will be most surely exacted in these changed hearts. A murderer on his way to execution may spit at the hangman, but a murderer whose heart has been cleansed by the burning fire of love sees the enormity of his crime and suffers accordingly. He becomes, in a sense, his own judge and executioner.

It would have been easier to awaken the queen to the real situation than it would have been to make it clear to Hamlet. The pathos of it all is that Hamlet was the very man to accomplish it, if he had known—Christ crucified.

The Gift of Calvary It is not a Shakespearean character we are considering. It is ourselves. Egotists, we lament that so much depends on us. Beaten in our tragic, solitary enterprises, we cower beneath what we call Fate, and cry we are nothing and there is no meaning anywhere. We vacillate and come back again to our old target, until at last our little life ends in futility.

Let us go with the others who might be called Hamlet to the Cross of Jesus.

There can be no egotism on Calvary. ' Daughters of Jerusalem, weep not for Me, but weep for yourselves and your children,' He said as He went to death, and in dying He cried out, 'Father, forgive them, for they know not what they do.' Will not this self-forgetting Love reduce us all to ciphers ? Look again at Him who hangs there. Is there anything that suggests He became nothing ? The centuries roll back the answer from a myriad minds, a million books, and countless lives uplifted by His uplifting.

How many men have died—many unjustly—reviling those who slew them, and seeking every way of escape ! Their names are forgotten.

Here is a way of life, Hamlet, which says, ' Love is better than hate,' and it lies not in a creed but a Cross.

He who hangs there is Love incarnate but invincible. Even the queen and Claudius He knows. Indeed, He hangs there that they may know He loves them still.

He offered you a goal that would have changed your vague wandering into a pilgrimage.

He offered you a courage that would have turned your defeats into victory.

He offered you Himself, which would have ended your loneliness.

He called to you from the Cross and He said, ' Son, behold thy mother.'

O Hamlet, if you had known !

Last year a man wandered London streets, in a vain search for work. There was no opening for him anywhere. He had no economic value to the community ! Walking along the Embankment, he saw an old man drowning in the Thames. Without a second's thought he jumped the parapet and plunged into the icy waters. Next day some one found him work. Within a month he died of pneumonia—the result of his heroic deed. Is there any sense in that ? Not in the laboratory of a materialist. Not in the Court of Denmark, where Hamlet seeks a lonely revenge. But if you climb the hill which is called Calvary you will find its meaning there—for hate ends in defeat, but love in victory.

III

MACBETH

Of the Vanity of them that would escape from God, seeing He is everywhere present.

Let them be converted and seek Thee; and behold, Thou art there in their heart, in the heart of those that confess to Thee, and cast themselves upon Thee, and weep in Thy bosom, after all their rugged ways. Then dost Thou graciously wipe away their tears, and they weep the more, and joy in weeping; even for that Thou, Lord—not man of flesh and blood, but—Thou, Lord, who madest them, dost renew them and console them.

But where was I, when I was seeking Thee? And Thou went before me, but I had departed even from myself; nor did I find myself, how much less Thee.

AUGUSTINE OF HIPPO
354-430

*For the Son of man came
to seek and to save
that which was lost.*

St. Luke xix. 10

III

MACBETH

THERE ARE FEW SIGHTS more tragic than that of a strong man acting weakly. Such a man was Macbeth. He had no subtleties in his weakness. Shakespeare's description of him is only half as long as his picture of Hamlet, yet it contains some of the most poignant poetry in the world.

When we see Everyman in this guise we are moved to profoundest pity. The contrast between what was and what might have been is almost unbearably sharp, but it is true to life. We must bear it! He who would bring good news of salvation must understand how Everyman was lost.

This is not a tragedy of imagination. The world has always had its Macbeths, and in its sentimental mood has looked about for means to save them. With a childish obstinacy it has refused to approach the Cross, and so the blood-stained hands have remained uncleansed.

Samson, that 'lonely pugilist,' was big enough,

DK

in his rugged strength, to make his fellows say, 'The Lord is here,' but he was weak enough to lose everything by his folly. The world's dictatorships have often ended so, and in the narrower limits of an ordinary life there lies similar tragedy. The history of the man in the street might become the story of a superman, but something happens, and he shrinks from potential gianthood to a frightened shadow on the edge of the grave.

The sense of 'lostness,' of which Maeterlinck speaks, seems to possess the Macbeths at a certain stage in their career. Murder is piled on murder, and the giant shrinks to the dimensions of a dwarf. Crime does not make the criminal great, nor sin the sinner.

In using Shakespeare as a guide to human nature one must remember that he has not the same value as a guide to the solution of its problems. He strips Macbeth and shows us the man in all his nakedness of soul. By his help we begin to understand the weakness which leads to ultimate loss, but he does not offer any hope of salvation as the tragedy hurries on to its conclusion. He maintains the supremacy of moral power, and he believes in what we should call 'conviction of sin,' when he speaks of 'the dagger of the mind.' He emphasizes the importance of the conscience as evidence of the virtues which go to make an ideal man. Self-control is always better than waywardness, and the true man must be just and loyal. Like many another moralist he agrees, as some one has said, that ' character not circumstance determines destiny.' All his tragedies teach great moral lessons, but he does not tell us what can be done for Macbeth when his sins are overwhelming him. He was a free man until the fatal hour when he made his tragic choice. What can we do for Macbeth in his bonds ?

There is no answer save at the Cross. Let us get to know this man, whom the world would say was lost.

The Weakness of the Strong Temptation suddenly meets him. The crown seems so near. If one or two people were removed, he might be king. There is no temptation at all in this, if one's values are right. If you are sure that a human life is sacred, you will not think of bartering it for a throne ! The devil has no more contact with a man whose values are right, but Macbeth is an easy prey. False standards become changing standards, and he ceases to make firm decisions. He is the kind of man who can be persuaded to make resolutions but has no resolution.

I remember going ashore in a boat manned by

boys from a training-ship. They wound a rope about a tree, but when we came back the boat was adrift and for a while we were marooned. The old cox who came to rescue us referred scornfully to the ' snowball-hitch ' we had given to the rope. Promises without resolution are like ropes that come undone under a strain, and resolution, in the last analysis, is of God.

The missing sentry. Any one might enter Macbeth's unguarded heart. He was not callous, perhaps not even ambitious for himself, but in that generous nature there was room for any kind of guest and all his luggage, however deadly it might be.

His resistance was negative. In his heart he hated the idea of evil gaining the mastery, but there was no indomitable love which possessed him. Lady Macbeth, if only you had held him— yet even that might have failed. There are moments in Everyman's life when the finest human love is overborne. There is no ally then, save God.

' *Let's set the stage.*' It is useless to resist when you are already toying with the apparatus that makes accomplishment a possibility. Everyman so often deceives himself that he is virtuous whilst he plays with the implements of sin. There is a modern colloquialism which describes such an attitude as ' being very near the edge.' It is much more than a question of nearness, because it involves the earliest sensations of the accomplishment. When a man opens a bottle and pours out a drink he is a good way towards drinking !

He yields to casuistry. When there is no guard at the door of Everyman's heart; when he has begun to toy with the idea that has been brought in; above all, when there is no supreme love which orders his defence,—it is an easy task to twist his conscience.

At first he has listened to the plot so attentively that his wife has shown him his part.

> To beguile the time,
> Look like the time ; bear welcome in your eye,
> Your hand, your tongue; look like the innocent flower,
> But be the serpent under't.

If Everyman had known the Love which went to the Cross, he would not have listened a moment to the details of his possible sin.

Presently, having half-consented, he hesitates, irresolute, on the edge !

> If it were done when 'tis done, then 'twere well
> It were done quickly . . .
>   that but this blow
> Might be the be-all and the end-all here.

In this mood of hesitation he declares he will not do the murder, and at the crisis he might have been saved—if he had known the positive love of God. Because such resistance as he offers has no deeper source than his own irresolute heart, he is listening again to Lady Macbeth. She jeers at him, making him feel he is committed beyond withdrawal. I have known men whose first sin was made, by devilish casuistry, the cause of subsequent ruin. Hear her as she taunts him :

> Art thou afeard
> To be the same in thine own act and valour
> As thou art in desire ?

'You have already committed the murder in your heart,' she seems to say. 'You may as well accomplish it.'

Once I met Everyman, filthy in word and deed. Years before, he had seen vicious pictures and dwelt on them. Presently he became convinced that he *was* vicious, and so added deed to thought. His life became a tragedy that need never have been. 'You cannot prevent the birds flying over your head, but you can prevent them nesting under your hat.'

The Battle Within There is a story told of a visitor to an asylum who had expected to see all kinds of obvious eccentricities. He was amazed at the normal appearance and ordinary conversation of the inmates. As he was talking to one of them he told him of his astonishment. 'Ah, but you don't see what's going on inside us,' was the reply.

When a man leaves the door unguarded, he admits friend and foe alike, until suddenly there is a strange civil war in his heart. He gets a glimpse, by the grace of God, of the battle within. When he knows it to be a battle, he is near what men have called conviction of sin. If he had known the Deliverer—but Macbeth was in his castle, longing for the darkness, on that strange day. There was an ominous stillness everywhere. It was an April 31st, on which anything might happen. And whilst his battle raged within, she who tempted him prayed her devil's prayer:

> Come, thick night,
> And pall thee in the dunnest smoke of hell,
> That my keen knife see not the wound it makes,
> Nor Heaven peep through the blanket of the dark,
> To cry, 'Hold, hold.'

So the darkness fell on castle walls and human hearts, until it shut out even the Cross.

The Lost Soul That is the penalty of human freedom. It can shroud the Cross so thickly that at last it cries out, 'There is no Cross, no Christ, no hope at all.'

The gate is shut. The pathos of the situation lies in the fact that it is not God but man who shuts the gate. Everyman, hag-haunted, but lately become a noble knight, is already a slayer of children. He cannot realize it, and for him there is the terror of being shut out—by God. He whispers, in his anguish, to his wife,

> One cried, ' God bless us,' and 'Amen ' the other;
> As they had seen me with these hangman's hands.
> Listening their fear, I could not say, ' Amen,'
> When they did say, ' God bless us.'

She answers him in his agony, as she might a child,

> Consider it not so deeply.

He turns like a wounded beast, unable to understand. He is perplexed not by God's cruelty but his own. He has shut himself out.

> But wherefore could not I pronounce ' Amen ' ?
> I had most need of blessing, and 'Amen '
> Stuck in my throat.

No sin can be undone. Macbeth, like many another man, is sure the door can never be opened to him again, because he is certain that God shut it. If he had known that he shut it himself, he might have believed in its re-opening from the other side. Instead, he approaches the pessimism of Omar Khayyám. ' There was a door to which I found no key.' It was Dean Inge who lit up the dark mystery when he said, ' Of course there was no key, because there was no lock on the door.' God does not lock the door against us, it is we who keep Love out.

Macbeth looks at the bloody hands which seem to have settled his fate eternally.

> What hands are here ? Ha ! they pluck out mine eyes.
> Will all great Neptune's ocean wash this blood
> Clean from my hand ? No, this my hand will rather
> The multitudinous seas incarnadine,
> Making the green one red.

It is not the colour of his hands, but their symbolism in his heart, which disturbs him. There seems to be no cure. Nothing—no one, not even God, can undo his sin. If he had known the secret of the Cross, he would have understood that ' God may sterilize the heart against its evil.' He would have known still more, that ' God can fertilize it, once again, for good.'

No natural cure for sin. ' Let us rule out the supernatural ' is one of the parrot-cries of to-day. It is shrieked at us from the soap-box platform in the market-place. It is clothed in elegant phrase by authors, who are clever enough to know the public likes a dash of morality, but who are terribly afraid of committing themselves to a belief in God.

When Everyman has sinned sufficiently ' seriously ' to despair of the mercy of man, they can only tell him that he ought not to have done it. Under certain circumstances, their last word is the gallows or the electric chair !

It would require a miracle to change the heart

of a murderer—and the word ' miracle ' is always spoken contemptuously. So the Macbeths look round for a way of escape and there is none.

No wish for a new beginning becomes a prayer if we have shut out God. No thought dare change to hope when faith is cast out. No deed of atonement has any avail, for the past cannot be undone; and, if we have not known the Cross, our yesterdays become an intolerable burden which crushes us. Those we have murdered in a thousand ways are better off, and we live on despairingly.

> Duncan is in his grave ;
> After life's fitful fever he sleeps well.
>
> .   .   .   .
>
> O, full of scorpions is my mind, dear wife.

And so with God shut out, the ' lostness ' becomes absolute to Macbeth.

The Averted Face   When Everyman feels thus compelled to face an inevitable future, he turns like a rat at bay. Even his accomplices fail him. He is quite alone.

> There's knocking at the gate; come, come, come, come, give me your hand. What's done cannot be undone.

But there is no sleep on such a verdict. He must go on, wide awake in his despair. For a moment, one feels, a word of hope is trembling to be spoken. The old doctor, so typical of those who feel that somewhere there is God, but that to locate Him is none of their business, cries out :

> Infected minds
> To their deaf pillows will disclose their secrets ;
> More needs she the divine than the physician.
> God, God forgive us all.

But it is too indefinite a prayer to mean anything to Macbeth. We have heard such ejaculations from distracted souls before, and they have been as inarticulate as a groan of pain. There is no sense of direction, because there is no real sense of God. Macbeth has lost all faith in himself, and God is withdrawn behind the gates of brass.

> I have lived long enough ; my way of life
> Is fall'n into the sere, the yellow leaf ;
> And that which should accompany old age,
> As honour, love, obedience, troops of friends,
> I must not look to have ; but in their stead,
> Curses, not loud but deep, mouth-honour, breath,
> Which the poor heart would fain deny, and dare not.

The old doctor has no medicine ' to minister to a mind diseased.' The cure, he says, lies in the patient's own hands. But Everyman has lost faith in himself, and he is convinced God has lost interest in him. Meanwhile God's Son hangs upon His lonely Cross.

Everyman is racked by memories—the written

troubles of the brain. They begin to crush him, and it is more than physical or mental pressure which has forced him to his knees. In despair we all cry out for the gift of forgetfulness. Since this is not forthcoming—and the more we desire to forget a particular memory the more indelibly it is imprinted—we are left with the problem of past sin. It is no use arguing that we must abandon ourselves to present happiness. Our past has come with us into the present. If we are to 'enjoy ourselves' to-day, we must deal coarsely and indeed callously with our memories unless there be some healing beyond the medicine of the doctor or the materialist. Duncan is in his grave, and Macbeth put him there. That act has changed Macbeth, and he must face the consequences.

To us it seems there are two possibilities. Either he may turn his face to the Cross with its message of infinite love reaching to the innocent victim and the guilty murderer, or, turning back, he may accept the situation as inevitable and die fighting or whining.

> Throw physic to the dogs, I'll none of it.
> Come, put mine armour on ; give me my staff.

That is Everyman in a frenzy of despair, yet maintaining some shred of greatness that was in him. For a moment, to a careless observer,

there is something fine about it. The sin has
been committed ; the human victim has suffered ;
this is unfortunate, but nothing can be done
about it ; let us go on to the end. We will
take the consequences and not whimper. That
is a modern attitude one meets constantly, but
it is based on falsehood. It is the way of the
beasts and has no sane purpose, no justice, no
mercy in it.

Sometimes Everyman, like Macbeth, is honest
about it. He realizes some of the implications
of his position.

> And all our yesterdays have lighted fools
> The way to dusty death.   Out, out, brief candle !
> Life's but a walking shadow, a poor player
> That struts and frets his hour upon the stage
> And then is heard no more ; it is a tale
> Told by an idiot, full of sound and fury,
> Signifying nothing.

That is almost true, but Everyman makes
one vital mistake in this mood. When Leo
Tolstoy was seeking a meaning for life itself,
he reached a crisis in which he saw what Macbeth
missed—' I then understood that my answer to
the question, " What is life ? " when I said that
life is " evil," was quite correct. The only mistake was, that that answer referred to my life,
but not to life in general. My life, a life of
indulgence and desires, was meaningless and

evil . . . and I understood the truth, which I afterwards found in the Gospels, that men love darkness rather than the light because their deeds are evil.'

To reach this point is to turn one's face again. In the dim remoteness one catches a gleam of God and, if one persists, one sees, close at hand, the Cross. Upon it hangs One whose supreme motive in that hour is to lead us to God, without whom life signifies nothing.

At this critical point, feeling utterly lost, Everyman turns away from the Love which was seeking through the dagger of his conscience to stab his spirit to wakefulness. 'Macbeth fails,' says John Masefield, 'because he interprets with his worldly mind things spiritually suggested to him.'

If he had known the love of Christ, would it have made any difference?

New Values It would have changed his sense of values in the beginning. No one appreciating Love on Calvary could dream that a throne was worth another man's life. The trap which presently caught him would have been powerless. So many of us live for years by false standards. Like Macbeth we fall into temptations which would have had no power, had our values been right. But when the die is cast, and the sin committed past undoing, what then? Our own reactions have settled the issue. Now we have time to think. Memory links up the episodes, and we do not know what to do with our yesterdays. We look behind, and lo, they have gone on before. 'I am the man who did that shameful thing.' If I look at the Cross now, what shall I find?

New Vision Perhaps I might get a new vision of God, seeking me because I am lost, because wherever I am, whatever I am, He loves me still.

Everyman shuts his little door, and by that very act builds a prison about his better self. If he but looks through a crack in the wall he will see that Figure patiently waiting to open the door that was bolted against Him. If he but beckons he will find God in the Crucified taking the initiative to break down the prison cell.

When we, like Macbeth, stand self-convicted, with red hands, and eyes redder still because of the bitterness of our regret, we do not seek abstract theories about the efficacy of the death on the Cross. It is useless to isolate it as an incident cunningly devised to provide blood-money for our sin. If Everyman, sinful and despairing, looks at the Crucified, he sees first the boundlessness of Love that is and was and evermore shall be. He cannot argue against that. Even his capacity for sin seems small compared with God's capacity for love. It was big enough to wound holy Love, free enough to shut it out—but neither big enough nor free enough to stop Love seeking. That is the revelation of the Crucified when Macbeth looks through the crack in the wall and sees the Cross empty, and the Christ, with pierced hands outstretched, waiting to open the door.

From that moment he may go on to know the rest—forgiveness, cleansing, a new birth and life eternal. He sees himself sought of God— to be saved, not damned. There will be much to learn, many things to suffer—Duncan is still in his grave—but hope begins with a vision of God seeking and saving that which was lost. Only when he sees God like that can Macbeth cease from fear or furious despair.

As Dr. Maltby has so finely said, 'We are bidden to believe on Him who, for the love He bore us, came to our help when we were "enemies," when we were "ungodly," when we were without strength ; and came all the way.'

If Macbeth had known that, he would have whispered from his self-created prison to God who waited to unlock the door.

There is an oft-quoted poem which tells of a

mother, coming on the wings of her great love, to the gates of hell. On the other side, souls in torment screamed in their agony, ' Let me out, let me out.' She, seeking the beloved, knocked at the pitiless gates and cried more loudly still, ' Let me in, let me in.'

If Everyman, deep sunk in sin, had known God as Christ showed Him to us all, he would have heard Him saying, even to the end, ' Let Me in.'

He did not know, he would not look. He would not die complaining.

> Blow, wind ! come, wrack !
> At least we'll die with harness on our back.

There was no more to be said. There *is* no more to be said if man does not know the love which comes all the way and, suffering death upon the journey, rises to go a-seeking even Macbeth.

IV

SIR LANCELOT

He that one sin in conscience keeps
    When he to quiet goes,
More vent'rous is than he that sleeps
    With twenty mortal foes.

from WILLIAM BYRD'S
Psalms, Songs, and Sonnets,
1611

Lord, behold my needs which I know not myself; see and do according to Thy tender mercy. Smite or heal; depress me, or raise me up; I adore all Thy purposes without knowing them; I am silent; I offer myself in sacrifice; I yield myself to Thee; I would have no other desire than to accomplish Thy will. Teach me to pray. Pray Thyself in me. AMEN.

(from a prayer of FÉNELON)

But I have prayed for thee.

St. Luke xxii. 32

IV

SIR LANCELOT

THE ARTHURIAN SAGA has been sung for so many
centuries, in so many tongues and keys, that its
landscape is uncertain, and its figures move in
ghostly unreality before our eyes. In spite of a
hundred different interpretations and a maze of
allegorical puzzles, the characters are real enough.
It seems almost vandalism to strip them of their
medieval trappings or their Victorian roman-
ticism and theology, but when Everyman comes
in stark necessity to the Cross, he must come just
as he is, neither adorned nor disguised. That,
indeed, is a cardinal principle for every pilgrim
to Calvary.

Amongst the people we have been considering
there is one man whose nature is chivalrous and
whose intentions are good. He is a knight in
shining armour and the king's friend. No other
knight excels him in modesty or steadfast courage, but there is one blemish which presently
mars everything. He is a man of a thousand
virtues and one sin, and the light of his whole
life dies because of this deadly thing.

69

Some have said that Lancelot was a British sun-god, or a Celtic myth, or the creature of a Norman legend. To me he seems intensely modern and real. One meets him everywhere—part of what has been called ' the eternal triangle.' Popular dramatists and novelists still exaggerate his excellencies and minimize his sin, but I have found him, more than once, struggling desperately to free himself from the mire, and wondering if he could climb the hill to see the Cross.

Like Peter he is most faithful, and in a moment becomes most unfaithful. The resemblance ends there, for his sin is not the sudden result of mistaken enthusiasm. It is the treasured harvest of an accepted temptation. If we avoid the allegory in the later *Idylls of the King*, we may take Tennyson as our guide to the man himself, but when we feel we know him we shall not be satisfied until we have brought him to stand with all the others at the Cross. On that last stretch of the journey we shall have to find the way from where he is to where he wants to be.

The third party in the eternal triangle may hold himself justified by all the natural instincts of human love—but if he be true in his affection he will set out on his lonely journey to the Cross just because he loves. The real lover does not risk the beloved because it is more pleasant to be with her. There are times when renunciation is the supreme test of love.

A Man of This man is no matinée-idol. He is
One Sin gaunt and battle-scarred. His strength is lifted far above the brute. Never for one moment does he waver in his loyalty to the king, his friend, except in one circumstance—and so all other faithfulness is wrecked.

All sin wounds God. It may be that Everyman is beaten by some other kind of temptation altogether. That does not alter the situation. One sin wounds holy Love, for God suffers the wounding of all the world's sinning in Himself. Just as Lancelot's guilty love for Guinevere spoilt all the work of Arthur, so the single continuous sin of Everyman frustrates, in him, the purpose of the Cross.

No additional attempt to be loyal in every other thing will make up for disloyalty in the one thing. The cynical French playwright shows us a man who bought his wife a new dress whenever he felt he had been unfaithful to her. It is childish to imagine that we can buy licence in one direction by being assiduously amenable to discipline in every other direction. There is a logical reason for this.

Virtues intensify sin. The mere fact that the Lancelots are utterly loyal in all other ways faces

71

them with a terrible problem. Because he was so anxious to be true to Arthur, he was inevitably inclined to withhold something from Guinevere. On the other hand, because he was determined to be faithful to Guinevere he was bound to be less than loyal to Arthur.

> His honour rooted in dishonour stood,
> And faith unfaithful kept him falsely true.

There is only one cure for such divided loyalties. Lancelot must find some supreme and dominating loyalty, to which all the rest are subordinated. The problems of human love are often difficult, and they are never solved until one has discovered the Absolute Love which purifies and hallows all our human relationships, healing the hearts which are grievously wounded in the process. If Lancelot had known the Lover on the Cross, he would have found the solution to his problem. A lesser man would have been content to transfer his whole affection from the king to the queen, and so have avoided the battle in his own heart. He was too true a knight for that, and so he sought some other way.

In his analysis, Stopford Brooke stresses the moment when Guinevere is unjustly jealous of the innocent Elaine, and the second crisis when Arthur still believes his friend to be true to him.

In that hour, Lancelot, despairing of love that will not trust, suddenly sees a glimpse of the greater love and knows himself, in shame, for what he is. ' It is the commonest cry of weakness in the unhappy hours of passion to ask the gods to work a miracle. But what the will does not will to do the gods leave alone.'

He sets out to find the Holy Grail. Everyman, hugging in his breast the forbidden flower, still sets out on such a quest.

The Vision Blurred The miracle is not wrought. It is not a crude failing that dims his sight. Cowardice is foreign to his nature, for he is the ' flower of bravery.' He is not arrogant like lesser men. He does not claim the vision as a right—

> and in me there dwells
> No greatness, save it be some far-off touch
> Of greatness to know well I am not great :
> There is the man.

But a man does not see the Vision just because he is modest. One of the greatest difficulties for Lancelot was that he knew what purity was like, and in his heart there was an impure thing. It is true that the pure in heart see God, but, as Percy Ainsworth said, ' the impure in heart shall see everything but God.'

> O King, my friend, if friend of thine I be,
> Happier are those that welter in their sin,
> Swine in the mud, that cannot see for slime,
> Slime of the ditch ; but in me lived a sin
> So strange, of such a kind, that all of pure,
> Noble and knightly in me twined and clung
> Round that one sin, until the wholesome flower
> And poisonous grew together, each as each,
> Not to be pluck'd asunder.

Both flowers are in his heart as he sets out upon his quest. If a choice between the two were forced upon him, it would be more than likely he would cling to the forbidden bloom to the end.

This is not penitence, though the world often accepts it as such. We go out to seek the Vision, and, because we do not find it, we rail at God. Only one of the two thieves on Calvary recognized Jesus, for only one was repentant.

It was a terrible adventure for Lancelot. His divided mind weakened his sword-arm.

> Then was I beaten down by little men,
> Mean knights, to whom the moving of my sword
> And shadow of my spear had been enow
> To scare them from me once.

In the madness of despair he struggles on through mysteries and pain towards his goal. Surely God will grant him the miracle now. He is battered and bruised, but he does not complain. Fierce fires scorch him, but he does not turn back.

Life itself is of little value to him unless he wins this peace of God—but in his heart the two flowers are not plucked asunder.

And so at last he nears what seemed to be the goal. In a paroxysm of joy he batters his bruised and bleeding hands upon the door.

> O, yet methought I saw the Holy Grail,
> All pall'd in crimson samite, and around
> Great angels, awful shapes, and wings and eyes.
> And but for all my madness and my sin,
> And then my swooning, I had sworn I saw
> That which I saw ; but what I saw was veil'd
> And cover'd ; and this Quest was not for me.

More than once I have heard men say words like those. Some of them, men and women too, desired greatly the blessing of God. Sometimes they tore at their breasts to separate the flowers so closely intertwined, but even then they failed. If they had known that supreme Loyalty, they would have known that only the pierced hands of God Himself can wrest the evil from the good and cast it out.

Meanwhile Lancelot comes back, more forlorn and in deeper despair than before. His distressed mind is driven again to consider Guinevere. If he renounces her she will be miserable. How often has Everyman excused himself on that ground ! What is misery and happiness, O my Lancelot ? If you would really show your love to

Guinevere you will not taint her with the evil which blurred your sight and wounded God Himself. What would you offer her that she might be happy, Lancelot ? 'Everything,' I seem to hear him cry. Everything ! Beauty, Truth, Goodness, for example, and about her life the peace of God which surpasses all our dreams ? These things she cannot know whilst you and she are false to Arthur !

This is no smug counsel of perfection. It is for many a man a terrible sentence, which makes him curse God and cry out to die ; but it is the only way. If Lancelot had known the tender yearning of God over those three troubled souls, he might have discovered it himself.

The Vision Clearing There could be no clear knowledge of the loving purposes of God until there was a willingness to repent. A novelist may kill one of the three people in the triangle for his convenience. A railway accident or a cold east wind may solve the problem as far as he intends to pursue it ! In sentimental mood, he would mourn King Arthur, whilst quietly settling Lancelot and Guinevere in a suburban villa ! If he is very modern he will feel bound to involve Guinevere in a motor smash and leave Arthur and Lancelot glaring savagely at one another, or cynically going into partnership, big game hunting ! These tricks solve no problems at all.

For a few more steps we may take Tennyson as our guide, for his psychological diagnosis is not as out of date as some would have us to imagine.

After Lancelot confesses that the vision was veiled, he surrenders. He settles down, once more, to what many people to-day would say was inevitable. But that is not the end. His own passion becomes languorous. There is a fine sentence in Stopford Brooke's study which illuminates the whole situation. ' And as in all the heat of his feeble remorse and of his search for the Grail, he had never willed, but only wished, for righteousness, the failure of the spiritual excitement left him weaker than before, but less repentant.' That last phrase is the epitome of his tragedy. In that mood of diminishing penitence, he takes the forbidden flower in his hands again—but it has begun to fade ! It always does.

There are some orchids which display a daring brilliance for a short hour or two. Their perfume is overpowering, till suddenly they begin to wilt and die. The fragrance passes and a sense of nausea pervades the air about them.

Though the reaction was not quite so extreme in the case of Lancelot, yet it was equally undignified. Conscience affected him strangely. He can sit at the Last Tournament and see the laws of chivalry broken without raising a protest. Life has lost its reality for him, but he remains a knight. This is no vulgar story of abandonment. He is as true to Guinevere as he has ever been, and she to him. Sometimes their love flames up, as in the hour of farewell, but it has ceased to be a master passion. It was always a forbidden flower, and conscience has never left either of them in quiet possession.

At this point Tennyson begins to fail us as a guide to Lancelot. He leaves Guinevere and shows us one glimpse of the true knight as he refuses to fight Arthur, his friend. We are not criticizing poetry, we are trying to find a way for Lancelot to the Cross. In the later poems Tennyson does not help us so much, because he is trying to write allegorically for an ethical purpose. Arthur appears from two different view-points. That is not our concern. We are told in greater detail of Guinevere.

Whilst she and Lancelot are struggling, where is God? Somewhere I remember reading a phrase which I have remembered, though I have forgotten its origin. ' She overheard her son's *thoughts*,' the writer said. In all the agony of conflict through which these two passed, I think of God ' overhearing their thoughts.' If they had known—— !

To Guinevere, at last, there comes the revelation. All the time she had been near a greater love than she had deemed possible. How blind she had been.

When Arthur comes to see her that last time, in Almesbury, he does not chide. If Tennyson had let him say less he would have said more. It was no occasion for a public speech, nor do I believe Arthur could have made it. He looks at his penitent queen and says,

> Let no man dream but that I love thee still.
> Perchance, and so thou purify thy soul,
> And so thou lean on our fair father Christ,
> Hereafter in that world where all are pure
> We two may meet before high God, and thou
> Wilt spring to me, and claim me thine, and know
> I am thine husband—not a smaller soul,
> Nor Lancelot, nor another.

This is human love, nearing its best, but it is not all. It achieves something in the heart of Guinevere, for earthly love can do many things. As Arthur rides away, the queen cries out :

> I should have answer'd his farewell.
> His mercy choked me. Gone, my lord the King,
> My own true lord ! How dare I call him mine ?
>
> .   .   .   .
>
> Thou art the highest and most human too,
> Not Lancelot, nor another. . . .
>
> .   .   .   .
>
> We needs must love the highest when we see it,
> Not Lancelot, nor another.

Human love can bring us to this point, but still we are not at the Cross. Guinevere's experience shows her at last that Arthur's love endures even to extreme mercy. We cannot see the highest whilst we mean to sin again. Repentance and faith, men say, bring sight. So with Lancelot and Guinevere, so with Everyman, there is a willingness to accept the consequences of sin which begins to clear our vision.

Many years ago, I found myself by accident in a law-court where a girl was on trial for her life. She had killed her baby, whose father had fled from her in the hour of her need. Her lover, whom she had betrayed, was in the court. He pleaded for her. Presently she was discharged because of insufficient evidence. The lover rushed to the dock and carried her away to a new beginning. We stood up and cheered as men will when love is really triumphant. It is God we are cheering then, if we but knew— God who gives us poor mortals the power to love.

The Certainties that Dispel the Mist In a mood made up of poetry and personal experience, Tennyson brings the end of it all in a strange white mist, through which Arthur goes to his doom. It is inconclusive and unsatisfying. Vaguely we feel that Lancelot, more lonely than Arthur or Guinevere, finds pardon and peace. It is not a very clear solution to his problem. What can we do for Lancelot and Everyman his brother? What can they find at the Cross?

A dominating loyalty. If he had known that Love on Calvary, it would have harnessed all his conflicting loyalties. In absolute discipleship all other loves would have been sublimated to one joyous purpose.

I remember reading a character-study by Hamilton-Fyfe in which he wrote, 'Suffering has deepened and enriched his temperament. He has a far-off star to steer by.' That was what Lancelot needed. He set out to seek a cup touched by the hands of Jesus, and even on his search he divided his loyalty.

He might have set out to seek God, and the Christ would have been his companion on the way. If he had known such a friendship, he would have seen Guinevere happy in Arthur's love, and therein would have found great joy.

True love desires the highest happiness for the beloved, and that comes only as our little lives are dominated by the Life that gave itself to live again in us.

The Certainties of the Past The mist is not about the Cross when Love is crucified for Everyman. If he will but climb that hill, longing above all else to find God, he will know, as

Peter knew, that Christ is looking on him. For a moment he, too, will bow his head in utter shame. There is no shred of dignity left to us there, until we know.

Look back, Sir Lancelot, and see the God who made the stars that looked down upon you in Avalon. They change from brilliance to brilliance only to fade again and die in the unutterable silence of the universe. Why all the fuss of making them? Because God Himself is working out a purpose which is beyond space and time. He is vastly concerned about something—about some one who is immortal—about you.

When you struggled with your problem you were haunted by those glimpses of the eternal which were but half-visions. You did not doubt that for some there was the fullness of sight; you doubted yourself, for you could not believe that God was the irrepressible Benefactor, who would remember even you.

The **Certainties of the Future** When you have considered that wisdom and that purpose, which are part of an eternal plan, what will you say of the future, with your problems still to solve?

Do you believe that love conquers all? You have two loves, you say? That is impossible. Look again at the Cross. You can return to

Arthur and Guinevere now, without dishonour, for love to you will be a new, transfigured thing.

Lonelier now, you say? Never lonely again, my Lancelot. When Gounod was very young he said, 'I make music.' When he was a little older and knew Mozart better, he said, 'I and Mozart make music.' Still later he said, 'Mozart and I,' until at last he said, 'Mozart.'

If you know Him who hung upon a Cross to help you in your hour of anguish, you will hear Him say, 'But I have prayed for thee.' You will forget your little prayers with their reservations, and you will fling yourself upon His praying. That will be your greatest prayer of all. The flowers will be unplucked, and, strangely enough, even Guinevere will hold a gift from you more precious than she ever held before.

When Ole Bull, the virtuoso, played his violin to a spellbound Boston audience, they called him again and again. They could not be silenced. At last he came before them for the last time and held up his violin. 'It is not I,' he said, tapping the instrument. 'It's that. The storms of a thousand writers are coming out.'

Love is a better thing than hate or lust, my Lancelot. It is no subtle creed you learn—not a creed but a Cross.

Come yet a little nearer to Him who listened

to your thoughts. He says again, ' I have prayed for thee that thy faith fail not ; and do thou, when once thou hast turned again, strengthen thy brethren.' The mists have gone. The way is clear. Arthur and Guinevere await your coming. They need you, for you are a knight again.

V

DEMAS

The Christian's great conquest over the world is all contained in the mystery of Christ upon the Cross. It was there, and from thence, that He taught all Christians how they were to come out of, and conquer, the world, and what they were to do in order to be His disciples. And all the doctrines, sacraments, and institutions of the gospel are only so many explications of the meaning and applications of the benefit of this great mystery. And the state of Christianity implieth nothing else but an entire, absolute conformity to that spirit, which Christ showed in the mysterious sacrifice of Himself upon the Cross.

WILLIAM LAW
1686–1761

For Demas hath forsaken me,
having loved this present world.

2 TIMOTHY iv. 10

V

DEMAS

ONE NAME in the story of the world has become synonymous with treachery—the name Judas. It is no longer necessary to use the complete phrase ' Judas Iscariot which also betrayed Him.' To call a man ' a Judas ' is to describe him clearly enough.

In this respect, Demas has escaped lightly. It is true that Judas betrayed Jesus, and Demas only deserted Paul, but that does not excuse the difference in the sentences passed by the world on those two men. No one thinks of calling a traitor ' a Demas,' yet he was a person not unlike Judas Iscariot.

To desert God's servants may be to desert God! The man who left Paul in the hour of his need was a man who was deserting Jesus Christ also. You cannot be disloyal to man and remain loyal to God.

Nor can we make a vital distinction between the act of betrayal and that of desertion. To betray Jesus meant to desert Him. The details of the thirty pieces of silver accepted as blood-money, and of the intrigue with the wily priests, were only incidents in an act of desertion. It is possible to compass the death of an individual by merely leaving him in a moment of crisis. In this sense Everyman betrays His Lord when he deserts the servants of God. The lukewarm Christian is unpleasantly like Judas. In one matter he is almost worse ; Judas left his Master on the way to the Cross, but Demas turns his back upon Him as He hangs there.

There is no need to devise an imaginary romance about him. He is but an illustration of what sometimes passes for Christianity. Apparently he came with Luke from Thessalonica, which was probably his native town. His name is mentioned in three of Paul's epistles. On the first occasion he is included in the letter to Philemon amongst those who send personal greetings. ' Epaphras, my fellow prisoner in Christ Jesus, saluteth thee ; and so do Mark, Aristarchus, Demas, Luke, my fellow workers.' The second reference is in the Epistle to the Colossians, where Paul writes, ' Luke, the beloved physician, and Demas salute you.' Whether the two letters were written from Cæsarea or Rome, it is evident that Paul was a prisoner at the time, and it is probable that both epistles were carried by the same messenger. There is a distinct difference

in the ' setting ' for the naming of Demas.   In the
one case he is reckoned amongst Paul's fellow
workers ; in the other he is tersely remembered
in the phrase ' and Demas.'

Perhaps it was accidental.   As Jülicher said,
' Paul . . . had a right to give expression in his
letters to his passing moods,' but this sudden
change in temperature seems significant.   In any
case when Everyman is a ' Demas ' his progress
is marked by such stages.   First he is active and
enthusiastic—a partner in a great concern.   Then
he becomes a nonentity.   His body is present,
but his interests are no longer in the firm !   He
is worse than a sleeping partner ; he is posing
as a friend whilst he is considering desertion.

The third stage is described explicitly in Paul's
second letter to Timothy.   ' For Demas hath
forsaken me, having loved this present world,
and is departed unto Thessalonica.'   Paul is an
old man, in prison.   The conditions have
changed, and he is no longer comfortably housed.
About him there is a sense that the end is at hand.
He is not afraid, but he is wistful.   It is an hour
when friends mean so much.   One by one they
have left him.   There is tragic simplicity in his
words to Timothy.   ' Come to me as soon as
you can,' he says, ' for Demas has forsaken me
and gone back home'—home, while his friend lay
in a prison cell !

The personal abandonment would have been bad enough, but Paul was too stout a warrior to have made much of his own hardship. It is not the absence of Demas which breaks his heart, but rather the reason for his flight. He has left him because he ' loved this present world.' What does that mean ?

His Preferences It is not enough to say that he was afraid. Fear is never easy to analyse. In the mind of Demas there existed the possibility of a choice between staying with Paul and leaving him. Such a choice does not come suddenly. It was the climax of a series of less important decisions. Had the position been reversed, and Demas been the prisoner, can you imagine Paul calmly considering the prospect of leaving him to his fate ? The very idea seems absurd. This is because Paul had been choosing hard, lonely, and dangerous paths for many a year. He did not concentrate on the possible results to himself. Scourgings and imprisonments came, but he took them as they came, because his overwhelming purpose was the spreading of the knowledge of salvation. They were by-products, unpleasant in themselves, but of little account, so that he could preach Christ and Him crucified.

Demas, on the other hand, weighed up the

alternatives, balancing the main result of one course—immediate comfort—against the by-products of the other. If he had known—but he did not know—what Paul knew! His gradual desertion began with his cooling ardour and ended in his ignominious flight to Thessalonica. He had been establishing in his mind a curious scale of values, until he had developed preferences which made it quite clear what his course would be when he was faced with a drastic situation.

Comfort or Hardship It was rough and uncertain in Rome. No one in the little Christian community quite knew what was going to happen. Even if Paul were released he would probably start out again on some mad adventure. He would never settle down in comfortable obscurity. Why not? Because he had received his commission from the Crucified; because he had learnt the secret of God's saving grace, and because he knew the joy of winning men. This made him comfortable in adversity. For him there was a supreme joy in witnessing. He did not shrink from becoming a martyr— for martyrdom was in itself a witnessing.

But for Demas the early vision had grown dim. He had seen only a choice between comfort and discomfort. The thrill of saving men did not count against the soft cushions for body and mind.

The other day I stood in a crowded lecture-room in a northern university. The audience was strangely mixed. There were old country vicars and distinguished dignitaries of the Church, young students and old philosophers, women with a passion to learn and hard-driven parsons of a great industrial city. We had all come to meet a man from Central Africa. We heard him deliver a lucid interpretation of ancient philosophy and its modern development, but it was not that which held us spellbound. It was the man who was the heart of the message.

As I listened I thought of a spring morning many years ago when Albert Schweitzer was twenty-one. The glory of the day caught his unspoilt soul, and God spoke so that he could hear. There and then he made a vow. For nine years he would study and teach and preach, but after that he would leave all such work, to minister in some more direct way to humanity.

At thirty years of age he had become a brilliant musician, a theological authority, and a financial success. He did not forget his vow, made nine years before, nor did he try to re-interpret it. There was no new choice for him. He was ready to make his threefold sacrifice. It did not involve any inner argument, nor did he have to force himself to do his duty. Quite simply he obeyed the call of Love, and there was no struggle between Love and Duty. A missionary magazine lying on his desk told of the need for doctors in Central Africa. In a moment he saw a vision of sufferers mutely enduring the loneliness of leprosy, or perishing by the mysterious sleeping-sickness. The hour had come for his new adventure. ' To abandon the organ, to renounce the academic teaching—activities to which I had given my heart—and to lose my financial independence, relying for the rest of my life on the help of my friends '—that was his own description of his intention. He must first qualify as a doctor of medicine. Eighteen hours out of every twenty-four he worked, until he was equipped for his new service. There was no delay, no bargaining even with himself. Soon he was on the edge of the primeval forest. Hardship? There is no choice for him. The alternative simply does not exist. He does not sacrifice comfort because of duty ; he just obeys Love—and Love is the Comforter.

That was why he held us spellbound that night. It was not his eloquence. It was the man himself. Like Paul, he was Love's ambassador.

If you had known the thrill of that, O Demas, you had not played at choosing a comfort which depended on outward circumstance. If you had seen Paul's eyes light up at your coming to his cell, you would have known a joyful comfort that no easy lodging in Thessalonica ever gave you.

Home or Exile But you had so often remembered what you called home. To be in Rome or to tramp afoot with Paul on his journeying was to endure a conscious exile. There have been those who carried home within them. Whatever task honoured love was a task which built home about Paul's spirit. If you had known that, you would have understood that to be in Tarsus, when he should have been in Rome or Lystra or Corinth, would have been to shatter home for Paul. No exile of the body necessitated exile of the soul.

A man who depends on physical nearness for his experience of love is always threatened with its sudden ending.

> Often-times he feels
> The intolerable vastness bow him down,
> The awful homeless spaces scare his soul.

Paul would have felt this, not when he was in some remote place, but rather when he was an exile of love, because he had refused an opportunity to serve. Demas, going home, left Home.

During the Great War, men on the Western Front counted leave as the most precious gift they could receive. Relief from the filth and blood and tears lay in that magic word. I remember meeting a man on his way home. He had just come out of the trenches after a spell of fierce fighting. He was due for leave. I knew it before he told me, for it was written on his face. He said, half shyly, ' I'm sorry you're not coming with me, Padre. I'd like every bloke to have leave to-day.' Within half an hour he had heard of a pal whose wife was ill. Without a moment's hesitation he had given up his leave to him. The last I saw of him was as he shouldered his pack and trudged back up the line, going away from home. But was he ? There was no trace of exile on his face, and somehow I think the girl who had waited for him held him more nearly and more dearly in her heart that day.

Sometimes men think of Christ's life on earth as an exile whose supremely tragic climax came on the Cross. Yet it was there that He cried, ' Father, into Thy hands I commend My spirit.' There is a sense of the nearness of God in the cry ' into Thy hands.' He was never away from home, even on earth, for where the Father is, there the Son may reckon home.

But Demas could not know anything of that, for he had forsaken Paul and home and God, though he was on his way to Thessalonica.

95

Life or Death When a man becomes a slave to a slogan like 'personal safety' he loses all deep joy. 'He that will lose his life, the same shall save it.' Paul knew that was true as he went to his last imprisonment, but Demas could not understand such a saying on his unhindered way to the freedom of Thessalonica. He was seeking to save his life by that journey, but he was so limiting the definition of life that he was at the mercy of a thousand circumstances—a storm at sea, a brigand's murderous assault, or the private adventure of a microbe.

For Paul, 'life' meant something so different that neither fire-ball nor plague nor executioner's sword could touch it.

> I am persuaded that no thing shall sunder
> > Us from the love that saveth us from sin,
> Lift it or lose hereover or hereunder,
> > Pluck it hereout or strangle it herein.

He did not go to Rome or to prison to save his life by losing it. He went to Rome because Love called him. But in the secret loneliness of his cell he heard the Voice again, and it comforted him : 'He that will lose his life, the same shall save it, Paul, my son.'

'This paradox,' says Mr. Chesterton, 'is the whole principle of courage. . . . [A man] must seek his life in a spirit of furious indifference to it ; he must desire life like water and yet drink death like wine.'

If you had known that, Demas, you would have seen that the moment you turned your back on Paul you turned your back on Christ and thus on life. So one might continue to enumerate the alternatives which Everyman considers and the preferences he foolishly develops when he makes himself the centre of his universe.

Blind Hatred of Other-worldliness His attitude to all these details depended on his limited horizon. This world was but an ante-room to Paul ; this life but an episode. To Demas it was the ultimate boundary. There was no beyond. His pilgrimage could never get farther than Thessalonica, and the tragedy for such people is that they reach their destination !

If Everyman would look humbly at the Christ upon the Cross, he would know that true Christianity has its roots in otherworldliness. To try to be a Christian, and live in thought and action within the limits of this world, is to court failure. Christianity is not a scheme of safe living in a dangerous world ; it is a way of dangerous living in a world that offers safety to Demas on its own terms.

' The early Christians, however severe and awful their life may have been, felt it, above all, a liberation, an uplifting, a *Sursum corda.*' The writer of that sentence, R. L. Gales, says that he is always astonished by the union of the genial and the austere in them. That is true of Paul. There was no ' fun ' for Demas as he fled from Rome, for one cannot forget the people one deserts. There was far more ' fun '—to use a modernism—for the prisoner left behind, even though to-morrow would bring the sword. Every gleam of beauty is prophetic of absolute Beauty, and Paul was not shut in by the walls of his cell or the tissues of his body. If the sword fell the gate would open. Life was too big a thing for him to be afraid of death ; it was, in fact, eternal.

The Other Choice So far we have come with Demas on his way to Thessalonica. Did he turn back ? It is so difficult for Everyman who has seen the Cross, and called himself a Christian, to confess his failure and return to Calvary. He is inclined to be obstinate and proud—to hide himself in Thessalonica though his friend rot in a dungeon.

But the Cross still stands, its arms outspread invitingly, even to the Christian who deserted Christ. When Everyman has chosen comfort and home and life, misunderstanding all his values, God still pursues him with that untiring love.

DEMAS

There are countless men and women who have discovered the thrilling freedom of Love's bondage. When Stanley found Livingstone, he begged him to come home, leaving Africa to its dark devices. He refused, and the younger man was astonished. ' Is the old man cracked, or what ? ' he said. Presently he discovered the reason for his choice, and with the discovery came a new respect for Christianity. He saw, in Livingstone, the constant victory of spiritual power over physical conditions. Biotic energy in living organisms uses lower forms in physical and chemical manifestations. Psychic energy uses both the lower ' grades,' whilst spiritual energy commands all three. Men and women who have looked at the Crucified hear Him say once more, ' Fear not them which kill the body but are not able to kill the soul.' When you begin to understand His love you understand that saying, and a Roman prison has no terror for you any more.

So Paul is never undignified or crushed, even when he is shut up in narrow limits. He takes ' his bonds ' and makes them messengers. If Demas ever heard the letters Paul wrote from prison, they may have turned him back to look at Christ again.

Some time ago I came by road from Bath to London. It was a grey, misty day, but much of the road seemed golden to me. Everywhere the little brown mosses had flamed into bloom on the tops of the stone walls that flanked my way. The broken rocks were glorified. We crown the gold with grey, but we might crown the grey with gold.

If Everyman, be he Peter or Hamlet, Macbeth or Lancelot—or even Demas the renegade—will but come to that Cross, he shall find Christ's wounded Love a revelation. He shall know joy in sorrow, home in exile, life in death, for he shall know that Love conquers all things.

' It was by giving His life for the world that Jesus saved it ; and we cannot go very far, if our discipleship is genuine, before we realize that only a crucified life can serve.' Canon Raven leaves us in no doubt as to the secret of joyous living.

If Demas had known ! What a great sentence Paul might have written ! ' And Demas will stay by me till the Dawn.' I wonder if he did turn back.

VI

PALM SUNDAY

GOD'S NEED OF EVERYMAN

GOD'S LOVE AND MAN'S

He seeks for ours as we do seek for His ;
Nay, O my soul, ours is far more His bliss
Than His is ours ; at least it so doth seem
Both in His own and our esteem.

.   .   .   .   .   .

'Tis death, my soul, to be indifferent ;
Set forth thyself unto thy whole extent,
And all the glory of His passion prize,
Who for thee lives, who for thee dies.

THOMAS TRAHERNE
1637?–1674

VI

GOD'S NEED OF EVERYMAN [1]

ALL THROUGH HIS LIFE Jesus borrowed the common possessions of ordinary men. His cradle was a manger, lent for very pity of a poor pilgrim maid. He borrowed a boat to cross the Sea of Galilee—and he borrowed a boy's lunch to feed the hungry crowd that followed Him. He borrowed a roof and a bed—and at the end they laid His broken body in a borrowed grave.

The only thing He appears to have owned was a seamless robe which the soldiers took from Him and staked on the throw of the dice. The poverty of Christ was no chance happening. It was the epitome of God's invitation to man.

Every time the Lord borrowed, some man or woman lent! It was no accident that He had not a beast of His own on which to ride in triumph to Jerusalem. It was no accident, it was not merely a gesture of poverty, it was a God-given opportunity. An unknown man,

[1] The substance of this chapter was broadcast from St. Martin's in the Fields, and appeared in part in *St. Martin's Review*.

who owned an ass, lent it to Jesus and so shared in His journey to the Cross.

I want to talk to you to-night about God's need of you. We look into the record of our own lives, and the mere suggestion that we have aught God needs sounds almost a blasphemy.

How can the Creator require our consent to use anything He has created? When God gives He gives divinely, and when He made man free he was free indeed. That is why a nation may declare peace or war, a man may become a miser or a Francis of Assisi, a little child may smile in the face of a primrose or pull it to pieces. One of the tragic qualities of our humanity is that we are free to refuse even God's requests.

Even so, we wonder how He can want the things He made so perfectly, now that they are marred by clumsy hands and selfish purposes. How can God need me—a handful of dust animated by His breath and defiled by my abuse of the freedom He gave me?

Long years ago the Master borrowed a lowly beast of burden from a villager and made no secret of His need. ' If any one say unto you, Why do ye this? say ye, The Lord hath need of him.' The most momentous week in history began with this incident. It was God's request for man's service. The cattle on a thousand hills were His—yet He needed this man's gift.

Is it unreasonable to say that He needs you to perfect His plan?

How can we begin to explain the universe, if we leave man out? God is not a child playing with a toy. The immense stores of raw material in the world wait to be worked up into new products by the skill and industry of man. Since he is free, he is not an automatic factor compelled to achieve mechanical perfection. He is a free agent, becoming conscious of new values as he works. Gradually he discovers Beauty, Truth, and Goodness, and, in the adventure we call Life, he realizes Love reaching out beyond material frontiers, past the artificial limits of time, towards Eternity. Presently, he becomes aware of a plan, he begins to trace the operation of law in a world of potential order. He accepts the responsibility of partial control of these laws. The Lord, the Maker of the plan, had need of him.

Years ago a little child lived in a stable-yard in South London. He played in dingy streets until he was old enough to be an errand-boy delivering papers. The Lord had need of him. Eventually he gave to the world secrets on which has been built much of the scientific knowledge of to-day. Because of him, some of you are listening to this service in far distant places. His name was Michael Faraday. The wise men of the world consulted him, one of the greatest experimental philosophers who has ever lived. But every other Sunday, for twenty-seven years, he preached to a little congregation the unsearchable riches of God's love. The work he did was an act of co-operation with the God who made him. 'All my life,' he said, 'I struggle to bring every thought into captivity to Christ.'

Nothing restores a man's self-respect so quickly as the knowledge that he is useful to some one who is older or wiser or greater than he. That such an one believes in him in spite of obvious failures—still more that some one needs him in spite of abject surrenders—raises a man from the dust to stand upon his feet and live. Such self-respect is neither self-conceit nor self-sufficiency, and no man can serve God who refuses to believe in himself.

Why do we hesitate to believe God needs us ? Sometimes because the world says loudly it can get on very well without us. It places no economic value on our services. We are unemployed. I was in a valley the other day, where hundreds of men of twenty-two years of age had never been able to earn a penny since they left school. Am I to say that God has no need of them because society has failed to recognize their economic worth ? You could not worship a God who

only needed the well-fed and comfortably circum-
stanced. The very fact that these men are not
hopelessly embittered was a proof of an eternal
quality which God waits to use. There are
men, to-day, who have faced the loneliness and
hardship of unemployment for years, whom God
is using in the building of His Kingdom. He
needs them, not because they are unemployed,
but in spite of it.

It is not God's purpose that men should starve
in a world of plenty, nor is it God's plan that
nation should war against nation. We live in
desperate fear of one another, and selfishness
or distrust causes us to devote much of our best
intelligence and finest craftsmanship to making
the weapons of war. Poverty *is* preventable, and
war may be ended for ever. The Lord has given
to us, with our freedom, all the apparatus of
peace and plenty. God needs man to apply the
principles of eternal love to the business of daily
life—to work the apparatus—and so to establish
His abiding Kingdom.

Not very far from here, I watched some children at play. The smallest stood apart, disconso-
late. She was not in the game. A few minutes
after, as I passed again, she was still standing
there, but her face was lit up. 'I'm playing
now,' she said. 'What have you to do?' I
asked. 'Well, you see, I'm a beacon,' she

answered. ' The others can't cross without me.' Life's ways are crowded and its traffic swift. Ancient hates and prejudices, callous selfishness and stupid fears, block up the road. God takes men and women and little children and uses their obscure lives as beacons, crossing-places, by which the struggling pilgrim passes on towards his goal.

Perhaps you are old and grey with more than the burden of age ? You feel your day of usefulness is past.

> The years like great black oxen tread the world,
> And you are broken by their passing feet.

The Lord hath need of you. There is no living soul for whom He has not some plan. He needs healthy bodies, but He also needs mature minds and hearts tried in the furnace of affliction. He called William Blake from his cellar and his poverty to read to men the secrets of eternity, and He needs the loneliest man who listens, from the distant veld or the foot of the solitary hills.

Remember, once more, when Jesus began His last journey, He called for the help of an unknown man, and borrowed his beast that He might ride on His triumphal way.

There is a picture of the Crucifixion, painted by Tintoretto, which shows great crowds thronging the hill of Calvary. Christ hangs already upon the Cross. Workmen stolidly dig a hole in which to step another cross for a thief. The second malefactor, not yet bound, looks keenly round before his final agony. On the left a group of riders, men and women gaily dressed, stand out brilliantly against the sombre wind-blown trees and the melancholy sky. There, in the midst, hangs Jesus, crucified. Look at His face—you cannot see it, for it is bowed upon His breast and hidden in its own shadow. About His head is a halo, not gold but ashen grey.

Pushing his way through the crowd is a belated traveller, riding on an ass. Suddenly the beast sees a choice morsel lying in his path. Crisp, dry, withered palm-branches! Strewn fresh the previous Sunday by the excited and mistaken crowd, they lie trodden and befouled by passing feet—food for a beast.

Thus the tragedy of Palm Sunday is laid bare. They gave Him palms! He asked for their hearts! Palms wither. Bodies decay, but *you* live on. The Lord needs you, not your applause but your living personality, to work with Him in building an eternal Kingdom whose subjects shall be one great family.

I can imagine you saying, ' If only I had realized this before, I might have given myself, unspoilt, to Him.'

' God forget me,' we cry, until we learn a

better prayer. Even as Christ rides out again to that enduring Calvary, He cries, ' I need you still.' Then, ' God remember me,' I answer, ' not as I am, nor yet as people think I am, but as You know I may be.'

We are wounded and marred by an enemy within our hearts. We cannot share in God's great purposes unless He heal our wounds. That is why we need Him sorely.

I see again, to-night, a hospital in France where men whose features had been shattered by the devilries of war were sheltered from the common gaze. They could not see themselves, for all mirrors and bright metals were taken away— yet they knew. All they desired was death to free them from their hideous exile. No longer could they think of home or loved ones in their misery. There came to them a great surgeon. He was a man of another race, but, hour after hour, day after day, he worked, building up their broken features till at last they looked like men. I can still see the light which shone in their eyes when they knew they could look once more into the faces of those they loved without fear or shame. It was a resurrection glory. They had returned from the pit ! The surgeon died. He gave himself for their healing, and they came back to life again.

We need the healing hand of God on our own

battered and scarred souls. He needs us, and He waits to fit us again to serve, though we have deserved nothing save to be forgotten of men and of God.

Yet that would be a selfish gospel if it ended there. Those who hear Him call can no longer live in a little world. The frontiers raised by self must be destroyed. We need God, not only for our own soul's sake, but for the sake of 'the other fellow.'

No man can proclaim 'good news' until it has passed through the crucible of his own experience. You cannot expect your child or your friend to believe what you have not yourself tested. You may boast of your genius for friendship, but you cannot call yourself a true friend if you know you would have to stand dumb in the hour of your friend's spiritual extremity. The Lord needs you because of the other fellow, and you need God for the same reason. If your child asked you, in some last desperate crisis, the way to God, could you answer that you *knew*?

You need God to teach you how to use the tools He gives—how to harness the forces of Nature, how to rule your own soul for the proper distribution of its fruits, how to live with your brother unarmed and fearless, desiring his enduring joy.

You need God, not to win the applause of the world, but to share in God's plan of eternal redemption. It was an earthly triumph they offered Jesus, and He refused it triumphantly, setting His face deliberately towards the Cross. It was the only way then. It is the only way still. You need God because God needs you.

There is a little fishing village on the western coast which I have watched in many moods. Once I saw it on a summer's day when artists were painting its beauty; it was a joyous picture. Often I have seen it when the fishing-fleet has sailed in to dispose of their catch; it was a busy market then. But once I saw it when a storm had raged for days with relentless fury. The little battered fishing-boats fought their way back, and presently won the safety of the harbour. In that hour we knew it as a refuge and a home.

Now God may be to some a theory—even a beautiful picture. He may be to others a working-basis for life's commerce of deeds and ideas. But to the storm-tossed souls who fight manfully to bring home their ships, He is the Father in whose arms is safe harbourage. Maybe you need God most of all like that to-night.

There is in our hearts an elemental perception that our finiteness needs His infinity, our restlessness His rest. When we decide this, and act upon it, His Will is yoked to the soul's chariot of vital fire, and the Lord's need is satisfied, even in us.

We come back, this Passiontide, to the Cross. It stands, the symbol of the meeting-place of man and God. Those two straight lines, ours and God's, meet once at right angles, but they meet nowhere else, though we extend them to infinity. At that meeting-place waits Love Divine, the Eternal Christ of God.

From that Cross He makes His claim. All that is worthless in me shrinks before the Crucified. All that is fearful is cast out by that unswerving Love. There is no further argument. Love conquers all—even you and me.

Go out to a new life—and if any one shall ask you why, say, ' The Lord needed me.'

VII

GOOD FRIDAY

THE NAILS IN HIS HANDS

God gives us the Cross, and the Cross gives
us God.

MADAME GUYON
1648–1717

Christ when He died
    Deceived the Cross,
And on Death's side
    Threw all the loss.
The captive world awaked and found
The prisoners loose, the jailer bound.

  .   .   .   .   .

O strange mysterious strife
Of open death and hidden life!
When on the cross my King did bleed,
Life seem'd to die, Death died indeed.

RICHARD CRASHAW
1613?–1649

VII

THE NAILS IN HIS HANDS

Iᴛ ɪs ᴏɴʟʏ ᴛʜᴇ ʙʟɪɴᴅ, or those who are in the dark, who try to see with their finger-tips. ' Reach hither thy finger, and *behold* My hands,' is a strange request, but it is made by One who knew man's blindness so well that He went to the Cross to cure it. Even then humanity would not see.

We still reach out clumsy fingers to investigate spiritual mysteries. The secret does not lie finally in pierced hands, but in a spirit wounded unto death. Our hands grope blindly, and because He understands our blindness He meets us half-way. God does not hide Himself from those whose desire is right, even when their methods are wrong.

Because the emphasis has been laid on the externals of the Crucifixion, man has been blind to its deeper meaning.

Legends have sprung up from such mistakes. Vervain was held to be a sacred plant by the Romans because its leaves had certain healing properties. A Christian version stressed this by declaring that it was first found on Calvary, and that it was used to stanch the bleeding wounds of Christ. Would that have made Him glad ?

The poignant folk-tales of the robin have given the little bird sanctuary in men's minds. A French poem says he flew to the Crucified on Calvary and tried to peck away the crown of thorns, but by so doing made them the heavier, reddening his breast with blood the while. Another version gets nearer to the fundamental principle. The tiny bird flies to souls in torment, bringing drops of dew to cool their tortured lips. As he comes close to them the flames scorch his breast, so that he bears their red banners over his heart. That is a truer emphasis. The red breast is his reward. One does not end by lamenting the wounds. One presses past them to see love's purposes and know love's victory.

> Prayers of love like rain-drops fall,
>   Tears of pity are cooling dew,
> And dear to the heart of our Lord are all
>   Who suffer like Him in the good they do.

Beyond the nails and the cross of wood, behind the consequences of love outraged, lies Love supreme in its unalterable purposes and triumphant in its ultimate victory. To look at this is not to end overwhelmed by tears, but to rise up inflamed with hope that will not be denied.

Let us begin by looking simply at the externals,

so that with Augustine we may pass from things outside to things within, and from things within to things above.

I. THE NAILS

Some one Drove Them In But they did not fasten Him. He hung upon the Cross, unprotesting, because Love held Him there.

We, of a later day, with our self-contained creeds, seem again to bind Him. He does not protest, nor does He exclude Himself from the circle of our insufficient words. Because He loves us He binds Himself to our minds, little in themselves but less because we have made them so through ancient prejudice or modern self-confidence.

Sin does not nail Him to that Cross, though we too often say it does. Sinners drive in the nails, but Love brings Him to the nailing.

> Found guilty of excess of love,
> It was Thine own sweet will that tied
> Thee tighter far than helpless nails ;
> Jesus, our Love, is crucified.

It was that timeless, limitless love which bound Him to what men vaguely call Duty.

Our pathetic symbolism has struggled to express this in our common life. For centuries the officer has raised his sword-hilt to his lips in salute—a symbolic kissing of the cross in affirmation of his pledge to honour. When we desire to call particular attention to some truth upon the printed page we mark it with a dagger. It is the sign of the cross which seems to say— note this well, it is Truth. A few generations ago, every child's primer printed a ' criss-cross ' as the heading to each lesson—as though to say, ' The fear of the Lord is the beginning of wisdom.' The village cross in the market-place was intended to provide a pitch for the preaching friar whose message rang out to the chattering crowds in the midst of their bargaining—' Be fair, be true in all your dealings, and in justice remember mercy.'

The symbols have passed, but the Crucified remains, held not by the nails men drove, but first by the Love which brings Him to our little lives in self-forgetting pity.

Some one Drew Them Out But that did not set Him free. Love is always free—free enough to bind itself.

There is a character in *Wintersmoon* whom Hugh Walpole describes in a careful sentence. ' Life was what she wanted—to savour it fully, utterly, to the last intensity, never to miss a thing, never to escape an experience, that would be the ecstasy of enjoyment if it were not for morals and other people's feelings.' Nails could fasten such a life—indeed, it is fastened already, bound by the senses in a bondage it mistakes for freedom. Love is free enough to bind itself to considerateness and morality, just to pull out the nails that hold other people down. The Cross of Jesus is the symbol of freedom in its fullest and noblest range.

II. THE NAIL-PRINTS

The terrible moment in the life of Thomas was not when he expressed his doubt to the disciples, but rather when Jesus appeared and offered His pierced hands for identification. Love is not blind. Love sees behind the mask, beyond the silent questioning. Jesus saw into the heart of Thomas and made the offer without being asked.

'Reach hither thy finger and see My hands.' At that word the disciple knew it was he himself who had been blind. He was not unwilling to accept evidence. The one thing he wanted to believe more than anything else in the world was that Jesus was alive. 'Unless I see,' he seemed to say, 'I will not believe.' But what he really said was, 'Unless I see *with my fingers.*' It is the tragedy of the realist who is prepared to accept the evidence of torn hands, but counts as nothing the witness of a breaking heart.

The nail-prints were proof that a body was

maltreated, but there were nail-prints in the hands of the two thieves. It is the inner wounds to which men are blind. Jesus the Carpenter might be shamefully executed, but Jesus the Christ was crucified, not because His hands were pierced, but because His heart was broken.

It is said that the Empress Helena, the mother of Constantine, went to Golgotha to find the Cross. After long search she discovered three crosses and stood wondering which was the one she sought. At last she put it to the test by touching a sick man with each piece in turn. One healed him and she knew, beyond all doubting, which was the cross of Jesus.

Forget the medievalism, and remember the principle enshrined in the story. The test of the Presence is not in the nail-prints, but in the resultant of Love given a chance to act.

III. BEYOND THE NAILS—MY LORD

We gather round the Cross, and our hearts are sad. The stark spectacle of physical suffering has moved the world to sympathy. We consider the situation quietly and presently confess to one another, 'We drove the nails in. We drew the nails out, but we missed the Christ.'

No sentimental regret can set Him free. We missed the Christ—but He did not miss us !

Because He was determined to save us He

brought His body within the range of our hammer and nails. No lesser love could avail.

If we had relied on the proof of the nails we should still be left with our problem unsolved. There might have come to us a Greek salvation. We might have gone on our way chastened by the spectacle of an historic sacrifice, but we should have doubted its efficacy for all men. We might have cultivated a frame of mind which would have helped us to walk, as Gilbert Murray says, ' among the beauties and perils of the world, feeling the love, joy, anger, and the rest,' yet having that in our mind which saves. Professor Murray says that such a way of thinking would save us—and the whole situation. ' It saves the imminent evil from coming to be.'

That is not the great trouble. The evil has been. It made the nails and all the rest a necessity. It drove Love to the Cross, because Love would not leave us to our own tragic doom. If salvation be only a frame of mind—my frame of mind—what shall I say to my past? I cannot bury it, for it is already part of me.

We missed the Christ, but He did not miss us. He is inevitable. He ' tortures us with His implacable love.' Every step towards Calvary is saying, ' I will restore the years that the locust has eaten,' and we look wistfully, wondering still how it can be true.

We still persist in asking how it works—not whether it works. We grope for the nails to set Him free, and He is there before us, free enough to deliver us from the shackles forged yesterday.

He *has* taken the initiative—the nails in His hands tell of the sword in His heart. When we open our whole being to Him, His Love flows, a healing stream, into our subconsciousness. We cry out in wonder, not that He is alive, but that we are. ' I live, yet not I, but Christ liveth in me.' Where Christ dwells, sin cannot stay. It is swallowed up, like death, in victory—the victory of Love.

In a book written by A. W. Haslett, called *Unsolved Problems of Science*, the opening sentence reads, ' Scientists do not know (among other things) why sugar is sweet, why a steel girder is not a hundred or a thousand times stronger than it is, or why some summers are dry and others wet.' Yet no one doubts these facts. In an excellent chapter on ' The Unending Quest' the author says, ' Finally there is one other kind of ignorance for which science cannot rightly be blamed, for it is of the very essence of scientific method. The purpose of science is to analyse, to explain, and to control. But it is impossible to explain anything unless we have something else in terms of which to explain it.'

THE NAILS IN HIS HANDS

We cannot begin to explain the utter love of Christ except in terms of our own love. As our love increases, so should our explanation of His love. Thomas begins with that limited love which depends on the evidence of his senses. The offer of Jesus is immediately followed by the growth of his own love and consequently of his revelation.

We begin to know ourselves, and doubt for a moment returns to the attack. We cannot live up to this. We cannot keep our promises, or beat back temptation, or endure the supreme test of sorrow. That is perfectly true. We cannot, but He can, and He waits with that wounded heart to succour us. ' Not I, but Christ.'

When Lord Salisbury offered the see of Durham to Westcott he replied, ' In the prospect of such a charge every thought of fitness vanishes. There can be no fitness or unfitness, but simply absolute surrender. I think I can offer all ; and God will use the offering that I make.'

At last we own we cannot be satisfied with an identification that depends upon externals. Nor can we rest there until we know. God has watched us floundering amidst the sorrowful mysteries. He has heard us cry out for proof. Suddenly he gives it to us. ' I know your unbelief. You *shall* see the nail-prints.' *That gesture is the proof.*

' I know you for what you are—wretched souls anxious to believe on your own poor terms, like blind men groping.'

We had almost lost our chance. We draw back our hands. His great love has not turned away from our blind and ignorant desire. ' See My hands,' He cries.

' My Lord, my God, we have seen Thine heart.'

VIII

EASTER DAY

THE EARTHLY PARADISE

O! see so many worlds of barren years
Melted, and measured out in seas of tears ;
O! see the weary lids of wakeful hope
(Love's eastern windows) all wide ope
With curtains drawn,
To catch the daybreak of the dawn ;
O! dawn at last, long-look'd-for day,
Take thine own wings and come away.

RICHARD CRASHAW
1613 ?–1649

In hope of eternal life, which
God, who cannot lie, promised
before the world began.

Titus i. 2

EASTER DAY

VIII

THE EARTHLY PARADISE

SOMEWHERE IN THE MISTS about his little life, man has imagined the Happy Isles. The pagan peopled them with glad innocents, who lived for ever in sweet-scented gardens, sunny and secure. The secret way was hidden from the common gaze of man, but it was real enough to keep him peering wistfully into the shadows in an agony of desire. Since there was no escape from the mystery of death, as Virgil says, 'men were stretching out their hands in longing for the farther shore.' Sometimes the bystanders laughed in frivolous derision—'Hold all a mockery,' they said, 'for nothing is our own.' Sometimes they agreed with Aristotle that, when you reached the shores, you could not be happy because you would not know. Bewildered, many turned to the Eastern cults which invaded the Roman Empire. Here, in spite of emotional excesses, they were offered a hope of a life beyond, through the rigid observance of complicated ceremonial.

Then, quite suddenly, a challenge was presented to the world. A small group of people began to say definitely that their Master had risen from the dead. It was useless to argue with them. They were quite sure, and, indeed, their own transfigured lives were argument enough! They silenced debate, not by a philosophy, but by a life. Day after day they became more firmly convinced that Christ was with them, guiding and inspiring them in all they did. There was no longer a spirit of defeat or even disappointment in their attitude. The maddest enterprises appeared to them possibilities. They began to live ' in hope of eternal life,' not because they were performing mystic rites, or even starting mass movements, but because they knew Christ was risen. When they grew old, and came close to the mystery of death, they did not become morose or abandoned, nor were they stoics accepting the inevitable. Such an one as Paul the aged wrote to Titus ' in hope of eternal life which God . . . promised years ago.' There was a glow of happiness as they looked into the mists, and it led them to heights of joyful sacrifice which no psychological theory of ' wish-fulfilment ' can explain.

Sometimes their way ended in a martyrdom

which they welcomed, since it brought them more quickly to 'the haven of their desire.' The mob resented their hopefulness which amounted to certainty. They took the body of Polycarp and burnt it in the arena, but this little band of Christians looked in pity upon such efforts to destroy his immortal life, and wrote their account—' He was apprehended by Herodes, when Philip of Tralles was high priest, in the proconsulship of Statius Quadratus, but *in the reign of the everlasting King, Jesus Christ.*'

They lived in this conscious experience of an eternal kingdom, and for a time a martyr's death was the desire of many a heart. One can understand something of the thrill which such a constant possibility gave to their witness-bearing. Death lost its terrors and became the way to fuller life.

The tides of persecution ebbed, and, in the easier days which followed, age became a greyer process. Flames no longer lit the way. Life just drew remorselessly to its ending. There was no virtue in being old ; no virtue in dying.

Gradually ' Paradise ' became again a garden in men's thought. In spite of medieval extravagance the figure was not unsuitable. Man for ever seeks ' that other country with slenderer towers and more winding rivers, and trees like flowers, and with softer sunshine on more gracefully proportioned fields and ways, which the fancy of the exile and the pilgrim, and the schoolboy far from home, and of those kept at home unwillingly, everywhere builds up before and behind them.' The tragedy is that so many fear that it is but 'a fancy'—to use Walter Pater's word—and dread the sudden shattering of hope founded on a dream.

When William Morris planned a series of romantic tales he fitted them into a scheme which depended on this universal longing to discover some farther shore immune from death and disease. His travellers set out from Wick to escape the peril of the Black Death and to discover the Blessed Isles. Weary years of seeking brought them at last to a forgotten island where dwelt a lost race of Greek extraction. (For a moment the voyagers will serve us as typical of men who long to escape from life with its limitations and its dreads.) It had been a wearisome journey, and they had changed.

The men themselves are shrivelled, bent and gray ;
And as they lean upon their spears
Their brows seem furrowed deep with more than years
. . . Bent are they less with time than miseries.

Why did they ever set out ?

The Thing Feared Have you ever read of the Black Death? That was its colour, and it is the quality of impenetrable darkness which men still dread.

Death have we hated, knowing not what it meant ;
Life have we loved through green leaf and through sere,
Though still the less we knew of its intent.

Why do we hate death ? It is inexorable in its demands. No physician may win a final victory against this adversary. It ends childhood with a sudden blow and cuts short the artist's skill as it reaches maturity. Love in its most unselfish expression is quickly silenced. Men long to slay this dreadful foe, so obscure, so mysterious. We look about us as wildly as did those ancients setting sail from Wick. Love stands helpless, and when the beloved is snatched away knows life can never be the same again.

Youth shrugs its shoulders. The journey is only beginning. Why think about its ending ? The morning is sunny. There is a heat mist everywhere. We cannot see very plainly, but we are going on. Life calls. Whoever else may die—we are immortal, for a little while !

The mid-years, like mid-day, are clearer. We have to think, and we fear the Thing, though we scorn to speak of it to one another. Sometimes our actions screen us. Stoically we go on, taking risks now and again, to make our fellows think we do not care. We find a strange distraction in work. As Hilaire Belloc says of such a man, ' the equilibrium of his soul is only to be discovered in marching and continually marching.'

But we cannot keep on with that rhythmic tramp for ever. We grow weary ; our steps slow down, and the inevitable end draws near. What then ?

How we hate death ! We may snarl at the suggestion, declaring that we are indifferent, but the mere fact that we are forced to admit its final victory alters the whole tenor of our lives. We may answer our own doubts by saying we do not know, but even so we rob life of its gay anticipation. Such an one as Paul the aged is writing ' in hope of eternal life.' Is it merely an old man's pious hope ? Many a year before, he swung along rough roads and stood unflinchingly before angry multitudes, because he neither hated nor feared death.

Few men have been more sane than James Smetham, as he faced the situation. ' Life ceases so silently,' he says. ' We have no power over those we loved most. They *will* slide from us and pass into darkness. What peace can there be in death, either to the dying, or the witness of it, but that which comes from the possession of faith ? There may be stoicism, but not peace. . . . No one *can* be the same after the death of one very near to them ; they will either be much better or much worse, and surely then, when the hand of God is stretched out to resume a soul, the ear of God is very near and very open, and His voice very clear in saying, " What can I do for thee ? " '

But the travellers peering through the mists of the Atlantic for the Blessed Isles did not know this. They were sure of one thing only—that they hated death and fled from it. In our hearts we do the same—until we know. We seek some fastness so remote that death cannot find us— at any rate for a long time. What are we really seeking ?

The Thing Desired Much medieval thought looked for an eternity of changelessness. That phase has passed. We long for life that shall be progressive but not terminable.

The man of yesterday dreamed of some unknown land—a garden of the Hesperides— beyond the Pillars of Hercules, but in his heart he feared it was but a dream. The Celt stood on his rock-bound shore, looking out through the sea-wrack and the mists which shrouded it, and wondered vaguely of a land beyond. That strange country must be deathless—but the mists were for ever hiding it from his eyes.

It is man's uncanny desire to discover a spiritual interpretation of life. They looked for a city of life—but they did not know its builder and architect was God. So we, like Lawrence the Swabian and Nicholas the Breton, run away, and leave our fellows to the Black Death. No wonder we

135

grow bent with miseries of ageing body and unsatisfied mind.   Yet we do desire that knowledge of life which should be an answer to death.

Somewhere in our hearts there stirs a reaction to Beauty.   It is so definite that in exalted mood we cry out, ' That which moves me to the depths is eternal.'

> O beauty lone and like a candle clear
> In this dark country of the world.

We cannot believe that it, too, is the prisoner of death.   Surely it is prophetic of some utter Beauty which is infinite and eternal.   Surely, too, that within us which gave it such glad welcome is its kinsman.   Can that be destroyed ?   So we begin to think of eternal values in Truth and Goodness.   These moods help us, but they do not finally convince.   Many a man has thrilled to great music, only to fall back again into despair, declaring, as Father Wagget said, that it is but horsehair scraping on catgut.

Still seeking the Blessed Isles, we catch a glimpse of something in the glory of earth and sea and sky.   We feel with Wordsworth

> a sense sublime
> Of something far more deeply interfused,
> Whose dwelling is the light of setting suns,
> And the round ocean and the living air
> And the blue sky, and in the mind of man.

Yet even here it is but an intimation of immortality. Indeed, sometimes it quickens us to a more passionate hatred of death and a more hopeless desire of unending life.

We turn from Nature and the face of man to look into our own hearts. There is something within us which continually reproves our lower purposes. It will not be satisfied with our second best. Again and again it whispers, ' Higher,' when we would like to sink in protest against all further effort. This upward urge will not be smothered, and we ask ourselves why this thing should be. If life be compelled at last to yield to death, why should there be within me that which calls me on to some point farther than I can see—beyond the boundary of life and death ?

At last we look into each other's hearts, for there is that within human relationships which shouts defiance at our doubts. The love which will face death for the beloved, expecting no return, is a thing so wonderful that if death end it, then death is God and God is death. We will not worship, for we can only hate that which destroys us because we love. Why, in such a case, should we possess the capacity to love ? Can we believe it to be a sadistic device, created for the gratification of some unseen Power's lust for cruelty ? Did Christ suffer because the God

behind all things liked to watch Him die ?   Love
is not an economic or social necessity.   It is a
gift from the unseen, and if its cords be severed
finally in death, then He who first gave it is
either too weak or too unloving to prevent it.
If God be God, He must have an answer to death
—an answer which justifies the gift of love.

The Discovery of the Way   When Rolfe the Norseman and all his
companions had finished the telling
of tales, William Morris took stock
of the situation.   A year had passed on the
mysterious island, remote and lost.   The travellers had changed.   Death was no more a foe.

> With other eyes I think they needs must look
> On its real face, than when so long agone
> They thought that every good thing would be won,
> If they might win a refuge from it.

Poor travellers ! They had fled from death only
to find it in their flight.   Many a one had stayed
and ministered to the plague-stricken multitudes,
and, dying so, had entered into life.   There is
only one answer to death, but it is invincible.
Love conquers all things, even the last enemy.
Only as our search is prompted by love can we
discover the country where death is defeated.

' The kingdom of heaven is within you,' said
Jesus, and astonished the theologians.   There,

then, is the Garden of the Hesperides—there the Blessed Isles. Paul and Polycarp discovered this and walked fearlessly to death. Their faith was not a weapon to be used in one last desperate conflict. It was the atmosphere in which they lived. In Rome or Antioch they dwelt in an earthly paradise. Their thought and action was entirely altered when they lived ' in hope of eternal life,' and they had discovered the secret in Jesus the Crucified and Risen Christ.

There is a famous figure on the Sussex Downs which the country folk call the Wilmington Giant. The gigantic outline of a human body, with hands outstretched and clutching a staff, is formed of chalk. When the rubbish is scraped off, it is revealed as the image of a traveller pointing to the priory at the foot of the hill. Weary pilgrims knew, as they saw it, that they were near God's place of rest. There they might pause awhile, but only to press on again in the morning. In the human heart there is the insatiable desire for life. We may posture and pretend, crying out that we are blasé, that life bores us and we are not interested, but deep down beneath the rubbish we still find the desire to live. Even the theory that the suicide is seeking a way of escape from life breaks down. It is not life that wearies men, but certain conditions of life. At the root of every sane human being there is a desire to live. Death has no right to frustrate it. Is not the desire itself an indication that man is near its objective reality? Can we imagine a survival which justifies such a desire, if it excludes the persistence of personality?

If the universe is a mechanism, then the individual need not logically survive. Take another look at that Cross, O Everyman. It is a strange product for a mechanistic universe!

If God makes us puppets to shatter us in death, if He causes us to love and withers our love on the edge of the grave, He is not Love. On that hypothesis the individual need not expect to survive and would be stupid to worship. Let him curse such a God and die!

If God be Love, then the individual who loves must survive.

Listen to the Christ again. 'Because I live, ye shall live also.' There is the assurance of faith. It is no mathematical proof. If my belief in God were merely the product of a laboratory experiment I should not love Him, any more than I love a piece of potassium that helps me to believe in a chemical formula. On the other hand my faith in God is not the contradiction of any scientific truth.

When man believes that his life is not bounded by death he lives at his best. It is useless to say, as many have said, that our influence survives us and that should be enough. Take such a theory to its logical conclusion. This earth is running down. The day will come when it will be cold and lifeless. The last survivors, having gathered, presumably, all the influences of the ages into themselves, would still be faced with the same futility. It would be their problem then, just as it is our problem now, if we maintain that only our influence survives. Every struggle for truth and freedom, every battle for righteousness, all sacrifice and heroism would have been in vain. Life itself would be a tale told by an idiot, full of sound and fury signifying nothing. There are few people who believe this, though some are quite ready to write it.

God and the immortality of the soul are inseparably bound. If we believe in the One we must accept the other.

When Jesus has taught you to say, 'Our Father,' He has proved to you, for ever, the survival of the individual soul. You may try to pray to some nebulous Creative Force, but your prayer will not continue long and will consist of petitions only, which is a strangely unsatisfying form of prayer.

We cannot stay for ever gazing into the mist and dreaming of the Happy Isles. We have to give some answer to the mother who mourns her babe and to the old man who dreads the coming darkness. We cannot run from them crying, 'We do not know,' for that would be to leave them to Black Death.

There is only one place where we can hope to find our answer. Let us go to the Cross—but it is empty. So we must go to the grave, then, after all! No, that is empty too. Love is risen, they say. Who says it? There are a myriad names—Paul and Polycarp, Bernard and Francis, Anselm and Aquinas, Luther and Wesley, Faraday and Brewster—and these men were neither fools nor knaves. They did not live believing in some shadowy hinterland. They walked sturdily 'in the hope of eternal life,' and they took hold, boldly, on circumstance, transforming ugliness into beauty, falsehood into truth, evil into good—because they loved God, and death had no terror for them.

There is an earthly paradise wherever human hearts have opened their desolate rooms to His love.

> O heart in love, close cling to Him
> The risen Christ.